Sir George Alexander
and the St. James' Theatre

GEORGE ALEXANDER

[*Frontispiece*

Sir George Alexander

&

The St. James' Theatre

by
A. E. W. Mason

BENJAMIN BLOM  New York/London

First Published 1935
Reissued 1969 by
Benjamin Blom, Inc., Bronx, New York 10452
and 56 Doughty Street, London, W.C. 1

Library of Congress Catalog Card Number 73-82825

Printed in the United States of America

PREFACE

I BEG here to thank Dame Madge Kendal for allowing me to print a letter from the late W. H. Kendal;
Mrs Hughes for allowing me to print letters from
the late Sir Arthur Pinero; Captain Vyvyan Holland,
letters from the late Oscar Wilde; the Executors of
Henry James, O.M., and all other Executors who
have given me similar permissions.

There are two Appendices at the end of the
volume. The first gives a complete list of all the
plays produced at the St. James' Theatre by Sir
George Alexander, with the dates of production: the
second a list, as complete as I could make it, of plays
produced by other managements during Alexander's
tenancy.

A. E. W. MASON

CONTENTS

vii

ILLUSTRATIONS

CHAPTER I

THE St. James' Theatre on the 1st of January 1935 entered upon its centenary; and until it had passed middle age it was a place as harassed and experimental as a post-war country. There were, to be sure, bright passages in its history. Ristori and Rachel trailed their tragic robes upon its boards. There Henry Irving, as Rawdon Scudamore in Dion Boucicault's play, *Hunted Down*, under the management of Miss Herbert, made his first significant appearance in London. For eight years John Hare and the Kendals graced it with the lustre of their art. They produced there *The Falcon*, a one-act play by Lord Tennyson founded upon a story by Boccaccio, and the second of the Laureate's works to be presented on the stage. They were responsible too for *The Squire* and *The Hobby Horse*, the first full-length comedies of Arthur Pinero, who at this same theatre was to confer and acquire such high distinction in after years. But apart from those periods, the doors of the St. James' Theatre were as often shut as open. Managements went in and were shorn and went out. Strange entertainments called burlettas failed to entertain; and even the lions of Van Amburgh could not roar the public in. But in November of the year 1890, an actor thirty-two years

1918

of age, with no more than eleven years' professional experience, took the theatre over, held it until his death twenty-eight years later, and gave to it a high and lasting place in any history of the English stage.

No doubt the adventure was more possible then than it would be in these days. There were not half a dozen sub-lessees, all wanting something for nothing, between the owner of the theatre and the man who did the work. Salaries and rates alike were lower. A play could be acted to houses half full and pay its way until a successor was ready. But none the less, the long management of George Alexander was an achievement which required, beyond the actor's talents, the judgment and courage which go to the making of any prince of industry.

Alexander brought to his theatre a considered policy, but it would be wrong to infer that it had anything whatever to do with the kind of play which he meant to produce. A foolish and misleading phrase came into use in the Press. A play was or was not "a St. James' play". It generally was not, for the phrase was really only useful to a critic with an un-acted comedy in his pocket—and there was a large number of such in the 'nineties, as Alexander's corre-spondence shows. It was a useful weapon to them, because it stroked the manager whilst it smashed the play. But in truth there never was such a thing as a St. James' play. The theatre never specialised, and its repertory became wide enough to cover the whole catalogue of Polonius. Comedies, Shakespearian, modern and romantic, farces, dramas of the day and dramas in costume, tragedies in verse, and tragedies in prose, historical plays, plays of provincial life, pantomimes—all got their opportunity on the stage of the St. James', if only they were thought to be good enough of their kind.

Nevertheless Alexander had a definite policy. In the first place what he strove for was the proper balance of the play and not the predominance of the leading part. The best acting which could be obtained to set the theme fairly before the public was obtained. It will be seen again and again throughout this Memoir with what care, with how minute an examination, the cast was fixed. An old friend of Alexander, writing to him upon the anniversary of his twentieth year of management, exclaimed: "You have not only done great things yourself but you have given others a great chance of distinguishing themselves. I cannot think of a manager so unselfish." Irene Vanbrugh, Ethel Irving, Mrs Patrick Campbell, Fay Davis, Lilian Braithwaite, Henry Ainley, Harry Irving, Matheson Lang, Herbert Waring, H. V. Esmond, Sydney Valentine, C. M. Lowne, Allan Aynesworth, Alfred Bishop, Nigel Playfair, and a host of other actors of the highest ability were engaged to interpret a play and not to exploit a star. This star shone in a constellation.

A small incident occurred during the rehearsals of a play of my own called *The Witness for the Defence*, which illustrates more concisely than argument could do Alexander's point of view. He was in the middle of a scene with Ethel Irving when he stopped and stood with that doleful, harassed look which used to overspread his face when the bottom was dropping out of his world. From the stalls, I asked him what was the trouble. He replied:

"We're in the centre of the stage."

I was a little staggered, for I had never thought of actor-managers as people liable to be distressed upon finding themselves in that position. As a rule they drift by some process of magnetism inevitably towards it. But he explained.

"You see, we play to rather sophisticated audiences here, and if I'm in the centre of the stage they'll say, 'There of course is the actor-manager', and the illusion of your play's gone."

Neither he nor any member of his company was stinted of his moment, but he must make his profit of it somewhere else than in the centre of the St. James' stage. So the positions were altered and the scene played a little to one side. The audience, in a sentence, was to receive the full value of the play if it held value which good acting, thoughtful stage-management, and appropriate scenery could bring out.

There was a second principle in Alexander's theatrical faith, and one no less important. In the farewell speech which Mr Hare, as he was then, delivered at the St. James' Theatre on the dissolution of his partnership with the Kendals, he said:

It has been argued to our prejudice that we have favoured too much the productions of foreign authors; but I would ask you to remember that in the matter of plays, the demand has ever been greater than the supply and that the history of the English stage for many years has proved it to be incapable of being entirely independent of foreign work. I can safely say, however, that to England we have always turned first for the dramatic fare that we have placed before you. That we have not done more has been our misfortune; I would like to think not altogether our fault.

Those words were spoken on the night of July 1st, 1888, and within three years it was proved that the supply could be made equal to the demand. No one contemplating the brilliant records of Sir John Hare and the Kendals, whether in association or apart, can doubt that they were supremely anxious to enlist the help of English authors. Dame Madge Kendal, indeed, in making a presentation to Alexander on the conclusion of his twenty-fifth year of management, before a crowded audience at the St. James' Theatre, attributed the great pride which all of the theatrical calling took in his success mainly to his consistent faith in English authorship. But at the time when John Hare made his speech it was not so easy to translate faith in English authorship into actual English plays. The attitude of authors was one difficulty, the custom of the theatres another. There still lingered, for instance, amongst the managers of theatres a belief that it was undesirable that the public should know what actual cash the house held, how much of a crowded audience was "paper", how much money. And if the author was let into the secret, it would be a secret no longer. A whisper of failure would precipitate failure. It was preferable, therefore, to buy the play outright for a fixed sum and then trim it and shape it as the manager's judgment and the practice of rehearsals suggested. This was Sir Henry Irving's plan. In other cases, the author went upon the salary list of the theatre as Tom Robertson did with the Bancrofts in the Tottenham Court Road. The author had very likely been an actor himself like Robertson and R. C. Carton and Pinero. And though these gentlemen were responsible for brilliant and successful plays, the field was limited, the supply was not equal to the demand.

English authors, for their part, were suspicious of the stage; they were inclined to despise it, or to pretend to despise it. J. M. Barrie had not yet devoted his unique quality to the theatre. George Bernard Shaw's bicycle was only beginning to describe the astonishing curve which carried him through debates and arguments and the vociferous Societies to the popular triumphs of *Saint Joan* and *The Apple-Cart*. But not very many others were trying, or at all events trying openly. Their status had changed of late years. The Copyright Bill had been passed. The era of patronage was gone. The author of a book was no longer hired, except for some special and occasional commission. He took a royalty instead of a fee or a fixed salary. He stood in a more direct relation to the public. What he wrote went to his readers without alteration by a stage-manager. It went in the exact shape which he wanted. He stood or he fell by the work of his hand; and the reading public was widening like a circle in a pond. Magazines pullulated, publishers multiplied. Authors would have their work served hot in their own style of cooking first, and when the dish was cold, the stage could have the hash of an adaptation afterwards. The stage inevitably turned to France. There was the magic of French art, a little more vivid than it is to-day, and it was to be got cheap. Sardou with his prolific output and his genius for effect was the magician of the day. Tin under his touch became silver-gilt, and there was often metal more precious than tin. The rights of Sardou's plays could be bought outright for a modest sum, and the manager could then put the author's fees in his pocket. It would, for instance, be interesting to know how much in the way of author's fees Sir Squire Bancroft, the owner of the acting-rights of *Diplomacy*, received from the various revivals of that play.

Alexander brought to King Street, St. James', a fresh point of view and a generous spirit. He planned to build a theatre of high prestige and financial success upon the foundations of British authorship. To that end he went diligently out in search of authors. Having secured the sympathy and promises of the most famous playwrights, he sought the collaboration of men who had so far never dreamed of writing a play at all. John Davidson, for instance, the poet, alas, too soon forgotten, Miss Cholmondeley, Conan Doyle, Thomas Hardy, Stephen Phillips, and, later on, Arnold Bennett, John Galsworthy, Quiller-Couch, Max Beerbohm, E. V. Lucas, A. E. W. Mason, and H. G. Wells. They were invited to talk over any theme they might have in mind before they set pen to paper, so that disappointment might not follow. I know no manager to-day except Mr Basil Dean who so puts himself about. Indeed, the young playwright is now at a loss what to do with his play when he has written it, and sometimes, even when his play is accepted, he has to find the money for its production himself. It is surprising in how short a time the example of Alexander has been forgotten. For his policy brought to him prosperity and a most excellent name. Out of the sixty-two full-length and the nineteen one-act plays produced by him during his twenty-seven years of management only eight were of foreign origin; and when the final accounts were made up, it was seen that he had paid £6705 in commissions for and advances upon plays which dates and circumstances had compelled him to forgo. But none the less the policy paid hand over fist.

§

George Alexander Gibb Samson was born on June 19th, 1858, at or near to Reading. There is a possibility that he was actually born in a train, and if that is true, he was already predestined to play with success the part of John Worthing in *The Importance of Being Earnest*. For Worthing, though not born in a train, was deposited in a railway station cloak-room. In any case he was a born traveller, for he wrote to his father at the age of five from Bath and at the age of six from Carlisle, and to his mother at the age of ten from Bradford-on-Avon. He began his education at Clifton, continued it at Ealing, and completed it in Scotland. For he got the most of his education at the High School of Stirling. Two fragments of his studies still remain. An essay on Ovid written at the age of fourteen and a rhymed translation of a passage in Virgil's *Bucolics*. The essay is of an unimpeachable correctitude, the young critic concluding that Ovid is still remembered as one of the most luscious if one of the most indecent poets that the Augustan age ever produced. The rhymed translation was composed in the style of Pope when its author was one month short of fifteen years of age, and the astonishing feature of it for those who were compelled to decode his handwriting in later years was not so much his similarity to Pope as the admirable clearness of his calligraphy. For the rest, his attendance at school seems to have been irregular; but when he did attend, according to his old schoolmaster, Duncan MacDougall, his "amiable and manly manner was quite a power in the midst of many rough and untutored boys". Young Samson's father had an agency in the dry-goods trade which covered a good part of the western counties; and at the age of fifteen the boy went to London as a clerk in the office of Messrs Leaf, Son & Company of Old Change. He at once gave evidence of a characteristic which all his life was strong in him. He never let his friends go, and being a shrewd business man as well as an artist, he took care that as he progressed they should be made pleasantly aware of his advancement. He conducted a correspondence with Duncan Mac-Dougall, who was then approaching his seventieth year and looking forward to a period of *otium cum dignitate*. Duncan MacDougall's letters, written in the most elegant copperplate hand, belong to the days of circuitous phrases. London is always "the great Metropolis" and its business people "the merchant princes of the earth". The old gentleman was obviously flattered by the attentions of a favourite pupil and responds with affection. He regrets that the business hours in London are very long, but is satisfied that if only Alexander retains the *mens sana in corpore sano* he will become one of those merchant princes himself; as indeed he did. Duncan Mac-Dougall gives advice:

Avoid I entreat you the pernicious habit of smoking, the prevalent vice of the day. As to beer drinking to excess I need say nothing as I know by experience you are too much of a gentleman and have been trained too well ever to be guilty of so odious a crime.

Half a year later Duncan MacDougall is receiving and is returning good wishes for many delightful returns of "this gay and festive season".

At this time Alexander took part in an amateur dramatic performance given by the staff of the house at the St. James' Theatre in aid of the Royal Hospital for Consumption. Duncan MacDougall is "glad to find that your superior dramatic talent is devoted to so good a cause". He proceeds to gossip about his pupils and his fellow masters. Three of the former are now becoming ministers. Of one of the latter, Herr Boos, "we have got rid without a tear, and the Board hope to secure as his successor a M. Vignon of the Royal Academy, Inverness, a gentleman of the highest qualifications and unblemished reputation, he neither drinks nor smokes, nor teaches music nor shirks his duty". As a gentle reminder to his ex-pupil he underlines the word "smokes". The amateur dramatic performance seems to have been an annual affair, for two years later, in 1876, Mac-Dougall is acknowledging a programme and wishing for a bumper house. The old schoolmaster is a little troubled about the political situation:

The whole talk here, as with you, is peace or war, and I do hope the former may be the result under the able policy of Derby and Salisbury in whom even the Radicals have confidence. Gladstone has been most outrageous on the subject and his letter writing mania with Bright's inflammatory harangues are doing a world of mischief and playing into the hands of Russia in whose honour they place implicit confidence. Nous verrons.

There is but one more letter from Duncan Mac-Dougall. It was written after his pupil had taken to the stage as his profession and when the old gentleman was enjoying his *otium cum dignitate* very much indeed. The letter displays a breadth of view which seems a little surprising in a schoolmaster of those days. For whereas young Samson's father was so angry with his son for deserting the house of Leaf that for a time all communications ceased between them, Duncan MacDougall acknowledges some Press cuttings and a photograph with complete sympathy. The letter is dated March 9th, 1883, after Alexander had made an appearance as Romeo at the Court Theatre. "I take the deepest interest in your advancement in a profession so precarious and laborious, but fervently hope that you may not regret your decision to devote your talent to the stage where so many have made shipwreck and so few have reached the highest position with an unsullied reputation. I have been examining the papers", he writes, "to see any notice of the Court Theatre, but in our Scotch papers we seldom find any articles except on the Lyceum. I do wish you had been going to America with Irving and his company. . . . From boyhood I have had a strong dramatic bias and have seen the greatest actors of this century in their greatest characters." Duncan MacDougall is to be left here, enjoying his *otium cum dignitate* and no doubt receiving from time to time until his death news of the rapid advancement of his old pupil.

It was indeed extraordinarily rapid. In the autumn of 1879 he joined the repertory company of Ada Swanborough and W. H. Vernon at the Theatre

Royal, Nottingham, took the name of George Alexander, and appeared in *The Snowball* and other plays. During the tour the company acted at Bridge of Allan, where it was seen by Field-Marshal Sir Evelyn Wood. For a letter from the Field-Marshal, written thirty-four years afterwards, describes the pleasure which Alexander's performance gave to him and quotes a prediction of his future success. In October of the same year he was engaged by William Foulis for a company touring in the "Caste" comedies through the smaller towns of England at a salary of £2 : 10s. a week, to play juvenile lead. He opened with that company on Boxing Night of the year 1880, and within two months he received an offer from Tom Robertson, Junior, of the parent company to tour with him from April 19th until July 4th at a weekly salary of £3 : 10s. He so clearly justified this promotion that he was re-engaged by Tom Robertson for an autumn season at £5 a week and for the season of 1881 at £6. It was in the summer of that year that he made his London debut at the Court Theatre under the management of Mr Barrett, and in November he was engaged by Henry Irving to appear at the Lyceum as Caleb Deecie in a revival of Albery's comedy *The Two Roses* at a salary of seven guineas a week for six performances. Alexander hesitated to accept this engagement. He was inclined to think that he ought to stay in the provinces playing a variety of parts for some while longer and he explained his inexperience to Irving. Irving, however, was satisfied with his choice and overrode Alexander's scruples. Indeed he could hardly have chosen better. The character of the blind Caleb Deecie is naturally sympathetic to any audience. "Nature has been your friend", a family acquaintance wrote to the young actor, and Alexander brought to the part on the night of December 26th, 1881, besides his good looks, a quiet sense of humour and a sort of gentle manliness—in fact, just that quality which old Duncan MacDougall had remarked in him when he was a boy. He was stalwart without being robustious, tender without mawkishness, and, though he appeared in a cast which included besides Henry Irving, William Terriss, Winifred Emery, Fanny Josephs, and David James the original "our Mr Jenkins", he made his own quite definite mark. Meanwhile he was persistently moving along, sending a copy of a criticism here and another one there amongst his old friends, and before the run of *The Two Roses* was over he was already in communication with Messrs Hare and Kendal, who were planning their season at the St. James' Theatre for the year 1883. On June 14th he was engaged to play the second parts to W. H. Kendal at a weekly salary of ten guineas, and was re-engaged by that same management on September 21st, 1883, at a salary of twelve guineas. During the next year he went back to the Lyceum to play in *Comedy and Tragedy* during Mary Anderson's season, and on July 19th he returned to Henry Irving. During the next six years he remained with Irving, occupying the position in the company hitherto held by William Terriss. He began at a salary of £20 with an additional one-sixth for each matinee, and ended with a salary of £45 with the same provision. They were

fateful years for Alexander, years of protracted rehearsals under a master's eye with an accompaniment
of criticism which could be devastating. The late
Norman McKinnel who made his London debut at
Drury Lane in *Dante* told me that the company
could predict the sort of rehearsal it was going to
have by the style of hat which Irving wore to it.
If he wore a shining silk hat, he was going to
be debonair and kind. If he wore a soft felt hat,
his "storm-hat", as it was called, his sou'wester in
fact, the weather was going to be trying to the
nerves. Norman McKinnel on his first rehearsal had
the misfortune to find his chief wearing his storm-
hat. He had to make his entrance alone as an old
man and without speaking a word totter right across
the rehearsal room, which was wider even than the
Lyceum stage. He tottered his best in a dead silence
past Irving seated in his chair with his storm-hat
on his head. When he reached the opposite wall
Irving said to him: "No, no, my boy. That won't
do! Ague, you know, not alcohol! Try it again!"
And he tottered across that room six times.

This, of course, was on a later day than when
Alexander was at the Lyceum, but Arthur Machen,
who acted at the St. James' Theatre, quoted in the
Evening News one of Alexander's recollections of
that period:

When I was at the Lyceum [he said], after five or six
hours of rehearsal by Irving I would go home almost crying.
I would tell my wife that I was afraid I had made a dreadful
mistake in going on the stage. And I made up my mind that
if I ever had a company of my own, I would let them down
pretty easy.

GEORGE ALEXANDER AS VALENTINE IN *FAUST*

It was no doubt a hard and anxious time. But on the other hand he was a constant witness of acting inspired by genius, and elaborated with infinite care. He saw spectacles in the grand style, he played a wide range of parts, and his shrewd Scotch mind took warning from the unhindered extravagance which reigned in the Lyceum Theatre from the portico to the stage door. He had one great but short-lived disappointment. In December 1885 he was cast for the small but showy part of Valentine in *Faust*. A well-known hero of the Sheridan comedies was preferred to him for the part of Faust. This relegation to a secondary position was a heart-breaking business for the young and ambitious actor; but he followed the example of Macready in his early days at Covent Garden, and he did his best in the one scene in which he appeared. H. B. Conway, the actor chosen to play Faust, was in bad health and after four performances he retired from the cast and never acted again. Alexander stepped into the part and played it for the rest of a run which for length in those days was unexampled.

§

There is no doubt that he had always set in front of himself as his goal the management of a theatre of his own, and in 1889 the project began to take a more definite shape. There was now no part for him at the Lyceum in Calmour's play, *The Amber Heart*. He moved from the Lyceum to the Adelphi and, while playing in the melodrama, *London Day by Day*, he rented the Avenue Theatre. He had secured a farce by Hamilton Aidé called *Dr. Bill*. The Gattis,

however, would not release him from his engagement in *London Day by Day*, so he put up *Dr. Bill*
with Fred Terry in the part which he would otherwise have played himself. *Dr. Bill* was an instant success, and when Alexander was able to join the cast it
lost nothing of its popularity. The second act closed
with a dance—the Kangaroo Dance. It is interesting
to note that amongst the congratulations which
Alexander received twenty-one years later when a
knighthood was conferred upon him was one from
Herman Finck, the well-known conductor at the
Palace Theatre, who was playing the first violin in
the orchestra at the Avenue, under the leadership of
Mr John Crook, when *Dr. Bill* with the Kangaroo
Dance took the town.

The season, however, was not to end without a
calamity. The manager of the Avenue Theatre bolted
to Mexico with the greater part of *Dr. Bill's* fees.
Dr. Bill, however, survived the theft. *The Struggle
for Life*, an adaptation of a play by Alphonse Daudet,
followed *Dr. Bill*, but was a failure. That was succeeded by *Sunlight and Shadow*, a comedy by R. C.
Carton, which just held its own. Alexander, who
had been told by Henry Irving that he could return to his old position at the Lyceum if after a
six months' trial of management he so preferred,
might well have been tempted now to accept that
offer. But whatever he lacked it was not courage.
He signed the lease for the St. James' Theatre in
November 1890, installed electric light there, re-
upholstered the seats, and became definitely that
object of so much debate, an actor-manager.

CHAPTER II

The actor-manager · The position of the theatre in the
'90's compared with its position to-day · The preparation of a play at the St. James' · Alexander's consideration for his company · His first production at the
St. James' Theatre: *The Idler*

IT is difficult for a younger generation to understand the winds of acrimony which beat about the
head of an actor-manager in the '90's; and they were
not blown up by a bellows. They rose from a genuine
passion. The Theatre held a more important place
then in the cultural life of the nation than it does
to-day. The great characters of the Elizabethan
dramatists, which demand at once the very deeps of
emotion and a close intellectual analysis to control
them, were more frequently seen upon the stage.
The public was more familiar with the plays and
took a greater interest in a comparison of the players.
Criticism was more subtle. The coming change
which was destined to confer upon the race more
of Mr MacDougall's *mens sana in corpore sano* had
only shown itself as yet too faintly to affect the
accustomed mode of life. Summer time was not yet
invented. Golf courses were still sparse; Wimbledon
was still more of a suburb than the playground of
Europe. No one danced between the courses of
dinner; there were no Night Clubs to which you
took your wife; Bridge had not gagged the wits and
the bores with an indiscriminate hand; and the

17

cinema had not yet made its alluring appeal. The theatre was *the* entertainment. Nowadays at a dinner-party you are more likely to hear the new film discussed than the new play. Then the platinum blonde had not bleached and plastered her locks; dogs were not yet horses; and the Great War lay hidden in the mists of the future. The play was the excitement and the relaxation. Now it is one of many.

The bubble boom which followed upon the war added its influence to the changes in the national way of life. Men whom accident rather than foresight had lifted for a brief while into an unexpected prosperity found a pleasant evasion from the Excess Profits Tax in backing plays. Theatre after theatre could have taken its device from the "In and Out" Club in Piccadilly; and still the aspiring backers stood in a queue. Under the stress of inflated rentals, salaries based upon the assumption that the run of the play would hardly outlast the period of rehearsals, plays chosen by men who had no gift to visualise them as they read them, and the narrow purse of the public, the position of the actor-manager became precarious. So precarious indeed that the gallant and able Gladys Cooper has no longer a theatre of her own. The actor-manager to-day is an oddity. But in the '90's he was so prominent and debatable a personage that that stately periodical *The Nineteenth Century* opened its pages to a symposium as to whether he ought to exist or die. George Alexander, the young Marcellus of his craft, was invited by James Knowles, the editor and proprietor, to contribute his views, but he was then preparing for his migration from the Avenue Theatre to the

St. James' and had other work upon his hands. By
one argument the actor-manager was a commercial
figure and the bane of art. He was jealous; Edmund
Kean would not act with Macready; Booth smashed
Macready's last American tour with a fatal riot. He
chose plays with an eye only to the leading part;
they satisfied his vanity, but they destroyed the
prestige of the theatre. Thus one side. Mr John Galsworthy, at a later date, accepted the argument. He
wrote to Sir George Alexander on April 14th, 1913:

You were, as you say, so very kind as to ask me to write
for your theatre. I have received such requests from other
leading actor-managers, but I cannot honestly believe that
any play I have written would have been accepted on the
condition that I might cast it as I thought it should be cast
(without extravagance) to get out the essence of the play.
Actor-managers, I take it, are nearly all in management as
lovers of the theatre, and believers in themselves—some of
them obviously magnetic and charming personalities rather
than interpreters. Why should they put on plays in which
the leading parts are cast as the author feels they should be
cast? . . . You yourself are the attraction to half the public,
and half the commercial value of the play. Whatever you
may wish to do you have always that fact before you. What
I have always before me is the essence of my play. How to
reconcile the two factors I have not yet discovered.

It is true that less than two years afterwards he
succeeded in making that reconciliation. For on
February 7th, 1915, Mr Galsworthy did propose to
Sir George Alexander that he should produce two
plays of his, *The Full Moon* and *The Little Man*.
But the earlier letter no doubt expressed his real view

on the question which so troubled patrons of the theatre in 1890.

On the other side stand one or two arguments most difficult to answer. There is nothing more chancy than the choice of a play. It requires the trained vision of a man who can see it in his mind acted whilst he reads it, and that gift is most likely to be found in a man whose instinct and intelligence and experience, working together, have brought him to the topmost rank. For no one on earth can tell what the fate of a play may be until the curtain has fallen upon the final scene. Expected failures have run the season through; expected triumphs have been withdrawn within the week. And so it always has been. On page 143 of the first volume of Macready's *Reminiscences* you can read his verdict:

From the many opportunities subsequently afforded me of testing the fallibility of opinion in these cases, the conclusion has been forced upon me that the most experienced judges cannot with certainty predict the effect in representation of plays which they may have read or even seen rehearsed. Some latent weakness, some deficient link in the chain of interest, imperceptible till in actual presence, will oftentimes balk hopes apparently based on the firmest principles and baffle judgments respected as oracular.

In actual presence are the vital words. The audience makes all the difference. It not only reveals errors, it discovers merits. It would hardly overshoot the truth to say that no play has been publicly given without the audience reacting in some totally unexpected way to a line, a piece of stage business, and even at times to a whole scene. The audience is, metaphorically speaking, a sleeping partner in the concern, and if the play be dull, literally one too. It becomes a kind of collaborator whose share neither actor nor author nor producer can foresee; a current passes from neighbour to neighbour in the seats, a fellowship is born, a play damned or made. It is a case of blind men on a road, but the one of them who has travelled the most roads and taken the fewest wrong turnings is the best guide. The actor-manager, too, has something else besides his financial prosperity to consider. He has his own good name. Herbert Tree, when he was asked what he thought of the prospects of Stephen Phillips' play *Ulysses*, answered, "It will be a very good play to go bankrupt on". Thus the other side.

But in truth, all these contentions for and against are a little beside the point. The argument that commerce is incompatible with art is false from top to bottom. The very great artists have never been averse to marketing their work to their best advantage. Great artists are full-blooded people who want all they can get out of life and want it with both hands. The more intense their concentration upon their art during the long days of labour, the more they seek that their rewards should be proportionately great. They may squander them or they may hoard them, but they want them first. I never heard that Cellini or Michael Angelo or Shakespeare were indifferent either to their fame or the weight of their pockets. The actor-manager is in the same case. The more complete the artist the more certainly he will want to be master and not man, to do things as he thinks they ought to be done, to control his

theatre in the way which suits his mind. The more
content he is to be a subordinate, the less likely he
is to reach the heights. That he may exercise his gifts
with that sort of spaciousness which is an attribute
of great art he cannot afford to treat commerce with
disdain. Indeed this compulsion of nature, for it is
no less, is likely to be more urgent in the actor than
in other artists; for merely to act in an age where a
play may run a year means too thin a life for any
man with the divine fire at his heart. Other artists
have their days full. The recently published Life of
Sir Gerald du Maurier by his daughter illustrates
with a painful insight the disillusionment which
comes from empty days. The film industry is bringing to-day the actor into a closer line with other
artists. But I am none the less sure that in the cycle
of time the actor-manager will return.

§

It will be appropriate at this moment to give a
first-hand account of the preparation of a play at the
St. James' Theatre. I had three plays produced by
George Alexander; one a failure, *Colonel Smith*, one
which made a moderate profit, *Open Windows*, and
one which was a considerable success, *The Witness
for the Defence*. I take that play from its inception.
I was first asked to think out a subject. Alexander
suggested to me that it might save trouble and disappointment if before I began to write it I talked it
over with him. I had in my mind an idea which
might crystallise if it was given time. For a year I
kept it simmering, taking it out of the pot every now
and then to have a look at it, and putting it back

again since it was obviously not ready. In the spring
of 1910 I had the theme, the characters, and the
sequence of scenes clear enough for narration, and
over luncheon at 17 Stratton Street, where I then lived,
I talked it over with Alexander. He was hopeful, and
during the summer I wrote it. I read it to Alexander
towards the end of November at his house in Pont
Street and he accepted it then and there. There was
nothing exceptional in that acceptance. It was his
belief that a decision ought to be taken after the play
was first read; that a second judgment made up of
hesitations and over-meditated doubts was much
more likely to be wrong. He was in the position of
an audience seeing the play for the first time; and for
an author it is one of the virtues of an actor-manager
that his play does not have to run the gauntlet of
half a dozen counsellors. As far as I remember we
discussed the cast at the same meeting. Miss Ethel
Irving, an actress remarkable for a combination of
delicacy and power, had then reached the high position which for some years had been her due. She
had a curiously appealing personality; there was a
natural gentleness, a pathos in her manner, and to
use the jargon of the stage, she "came over the footlights" immediately. The part of Stella Ballantyne
was probably the best in the play. It seemed to offer
more of emotional opportunity than the hero's part
did to the man. It was in those days more audacious.
I had myself a belief that the two characters would
be of equal worth to the players, but it was certain
that Alexander's would be the more difficult to sus-
tain and would certainly not stand out more than
the other. I dwell upon this because it is one of the

many confutations which Alexander's career provided of the creed that the actor-manager by the
compulsion of his position must seek to overshadow
every other character in the play. It was Alexander
who suggested Miss Ethel Irving. For the other parts
we secured Sydney Valentine, Alfred Bishop, Leslie
Faber, Liston Lyle, and Marie Linden, and the play
could not have been better cast.

A few weeks later I was called down in the morning to the St. James' Theatre, and in the long board-
room into which his dressing-room led I found a
small toy stage with a set of draughtsmen labelled
with the names of the different characters. For the
better part of two days we arranged and marked in
the script the various movements and positions of
all the characters throughout the progress of the
play. Alexander had analysed the dialogue sentence
by sentence, and every now and then he would turn
upon me with a quite disconcerting abruptness and
say, "What did you mean by that?"—disconcerting
because—and I had noticed it before—suddenly out
of a pair of familiar and friendly eyes a complete and
rather hostile stranger seemed to look at me. When
the movements had been arranged, what is known
as a stage cloth with the doors and entrances painted
upon it was prepared. Thus, before a single rehearsal was called we had a complete plan to work
upon, and anyone who has witnessed the medley
which those producers, whose mental processes lie
fallow until the company is gathered for the first
time upon the stage, have to disentangle will realise
how much time and discomfort were saved.

The rehearsals began at 11. The old-fashioned

ten minutes' grace was not conceded at the St. James'; they began punctually at 11 and ended at 2, for it was Alexander's belief that after three hours of attentive rehearsal you had got all the good you were going to get out of your company for that session. He was particular to break off at that hour. The welfare of his company was always one of his first considerations. Many of the cast lived at a distance from the theatres, they were acting at night, and they would be all the better for some hours of rest in their own homes. The only people to whom he did not show this consideration were himself and Ethel Irving. For on coming to the theatre once or twice before the rehearsal was timed to begin, I found them both going quickly through the strenuous scenes which they were to act together, whilst he suggested to her such movements, such small pieces of business, and even such intonations of the voice as seemed to him helpful to establish the individual authority of her part. There was never the slightest jealousy, never the slightest effort to diminish her. The play was the thing, and, but for his determination that no one at his theatre should stand in the centre of the stage, every opportunity was given to her to act him into the wings if she could.

There were two scenes required, one a marquee and the other a drawing-room in a rural district of England. As to the marquee Alexander said to me, "You know about that. You had better go and get the genuine thing." I discovered a firm close to London Bridge which made marquees for India. The manager of the firm said to me, "You don't want a marquee, you want the lining of a marquee", and that he provided and set. With regard to the second scene which, after the first act, stood for the rest of the play, Alexander said, "You can have a new scene if you like, but I've got one or two scenes in perfect condition which seem to me suitable. Each has been used once and some time ago. Come and look at the photographs, and if you like one of them I'll have it set for you. If you want a new one, you can have it." He showed me a photograph which represented the kind of room I wanted. He explained how he could throw back a certain portion of it to form a recess for the garden door; he had it set upon the stage, and after I had agreed that it would do perfectly well, he had it painted afresh. The result was that the scenery for *The Witness for the Defence* cost exactly £145 : 6 : 9. Alexander closed his theatre for four days before the first night, rehearsed morning and evening during those four days, had two dress-rehearsals, and raised the curtain on the first night exactly three weeks after the first rehearsal. Another instance of his consideration for his company is to be found in the order that no visitor should be admitted to the dressing-rooms of the theatre whilst the performance was going on. It was a rule very strictly kept, and the reason for its introduction was to prevent the cadging upon the members of his company by the many hangers-on who asked for loans which would never be repaid. His house was in order indeed. And letter after letter is to be found in his correspondence from actors and actresses who had served under his management thanking him for the courtesy and consideration which they had received. He had a staff proud of the theatre and de-

GEORGE ALEXANDER IN *MOLIÈRE*
A One-Act Play by Walter Frith

voted to him, as the following story shows. Amongst the leading ladies who made their name at his theatre there was one who at times indulged in a humour more splenetic than kindly. During a rehearsal this lady fainted, and Alexander, all sympathy, carried her from the stage to her dressing-room. A few days later she repeated the swooning process, and again Alexander responded. It happened, however, that the wardrobe mistress had noticed the lady wink as she was being carried off, and bubbling with indignation she took the information to her manager. Alexander said nothing, but when the lady fainted a third time he turned to his large and hefty stage carpenter and said, "Will you please remove this lady at once". She was up on her feet and rehearsing her part before the carpenter could get near her.

§

On February 26th of the year 1891 the first new play produced under Alexander's management had its opening night. It was a melodrama of the drawing-room, and we should find it, no doubt, a trifle musty to-day. It contained asides, unhelpful trimmings in the shape of an uxorious General and a sophisticated *ingénue*, and a trick to bring down a curtain straight from the factory of Sardou. Would Lady Harding go or not go to Mark Cross's bachelor rooms at 10 o'clock on the next night? The life of her husband was at stake and she adored him. If she would go, she must drop her bouquet. She must drop it before she left the party. Mark Cross, the man to whom she was to give the signal, was in the room. There was no reason why Lady Harding should not have consented with a nod, or refused with a shake of the head. There were others present, it is true, but she was never described as a fool. She could, without embarrassment, have crossed the room and in the course of conversation said "yes" or "no" with enough intention to show her meaning both to the audience and the character on the stage. But that would not do. No. She must drop her bouquet. So, when the suspense has been sufficiently prolonged, the bouquet is dropped and the curtain falls. It was a stage convention of the times that if an adoring husband found his wife's fan in a man's room, whatever of devotion and love she had up to that moment shown him, he must instantly conclude that she was that man's mistress, heap her high with insults, and propose a duel. The duel, and the bouquet, and the fan were stock pieces of mechanism, and in *The Idler* Haddon Chambers employed them all. The play, however, had qualities of a higher kind. It contained one very pleasant and tender duologue between a mother and a son; a strenuous and closely written scene between three men, and in the case of the American, Simeon Strong, and of the Idler, characters less obvious than were usual. This play was received with enthusiasm by the general public, but a great diversity among the critics. William Archer, a writer of melodrama himself, endured with difficulty melodrama in others. He condemned the play out of hand. Minds more liberal and urbane, like those of H. D. Traill, Stephen Coleridge, Lady Martin, and Edmund Yates, found in it fresh and nervous dialogue, a good deal of human nature, and a very moving conclusion. There was general agreement that Alexander himself had played an extremely difficult part with a tact and force which strengthened his grip upon the playgoer.

The play ran throughout the season to excellent houses, and prepared the way for the three successive plays which were to throw open not only the St. James' but all the theatres to the freer expression of ideas and to a natural treatment of them exempt from the tricks and traps and surprises which had for so long held the field. Characters were no longer to remain static, they were to develop under the pressure of circumstance. A neat effectiveness was to give way to truth. Those three plays were *Lady Windermere's Fan*, *Liberty Hall*, and *The Second Mrs Tanqueray*. It is to be remembered to Alexander's great credit that these plays were produced not at one of the small theatres supported by a subscription, where a group of superior people took the drama under its care. "The stage", Mrs Pearl Craigie wrote to him, "was never meant for six admirers, a syndicate, and the chimney corner." The three most influential plays of modern times saw the light in what was stigmatised as a commercial theatre.

CHAPTER III

OSCAR WILDE was born to write plays, but he did not at the first write them with ease. The art of the playwright demands an apprenticeship even from the most gifted. A novelist may, and times out of mind has, set out with no more than a group of characters, and caught his nitrogen from the air as he went along. It is at once his danger and his comfort that there are no rules to bind him. He can be as long as *Clarissa* or as short as *The Bridge of San Luis Rey*. A tact of a kind is his obligation. By it he stands or falls; and it is his own particular tact and not his neighbour's. A play, on the other hand, has its precise conditions. There is a limit of time within which it must be conducted to its end. The playwright's intention must be as clear as daylight to him before he sets his pen to paper. Otherwise his audience with the quick instinct of a crowd will immediately distrust him. He must know where he is going and step by step how to get there. Yet he himself must never seem to be getting there. His characters must be such and in such a relationship to one another that they arrive there unavoidably and by the compulsion of nature.

Lady Windermere's Fan fulfilled the conditions better than nine-tenths of the current plays even in

those days of Wilde's novitiate. But at times the
playwright was too obviously in evidence. He committed the crime forbidden at the St. James' Theatre;
he took the centre of the stage. Thus in Lord Dar-
lington's rooms he set the scene for fireworks. They
were admirable fireworks and they coruscated delightfully, but it was Oscar Wilde who touched them
off and not the characters. This is not to say that the
rest of the play lacked wit. On the contrary, there
was a bushel of it to the average playwright's peck.
But in the other scenes it shone more naturally and
with a less expected brilliancy. Here the stage was
deliberately set for witty passages, and the scene led
more than one spectator to crack an easy joke about
the output of "The Oscar Wilde Epigram and Para-
dox Company, Limited". But in fact Wilde's wit was
spontaneous. In any congenial company it played
without effort about whatever was the subject of the
talk. He never diverted the conversation to a topic
upon which he was prepared to be brilliant. Nor
did he seek to dominate it. He slipped into it. His
heavy cheeks and thick lips would become sensitive
and alert; a gaiety changed his face; he took the
ball which was thrown and tossed it back upon the
instant, but never so sharply that it hurt. For his
was the rarest wit, for it was without malice; it was
the readiest, for it had not to seek its occasion.

He had revisited Oxford when the O.U.D.S. produced the *Alcestes* of Euripides, and at supper after
the first performance I, who had been playing
Herakles, sat opposite to him. I met him afterwards
when I had come to London and was writing my
first book; and he said, no doubt with the thought

that a square meal might be useful, "There is always luncheon at 1 o'clock at the Café Royal". From time to time various young people gathered at his table. I remember Harry and Laurence Irving in particular, and at times William Heinemann. Wilde was always stimulating and kindly. He would listen to what we were doing, or trying to do, and offer here a criticism and there an encouragement; and his wit was always ready at his lips. I was writing a short novel which was afterwards published under the bad title of *A Romance of Wastdale*, and as I told him the story he shook his head. For instead of being a story about lovers, it was a story about a brother and sister.

"No", he said, nodding his head, "that won't do. Everything in life has its symbol. Passion has its flower. And affection between a brother and a sister has its symbol too. But, my dear fellow, it's cold boiled mutton."

On another occasion Heinemann was very annoyed because Richard Le Gallienne had published a book called *The Religion of a Literary Man*. He was extremely pettish about it. What was the difference, he wanted to know, between the religion of a literary man and anybody else's religion. Wilde gazed at Heinemann sorrowfully. "My dear fellow," he protested, nodding his head like a mandarin with his knuckles to his teeth, "how far you are behind the times! Of course Le Gallienne is right. He knows that nowadays a man's religion is a thing solely between himself—and the public."

It was at one of these luncheons, too, when someone spoke with triviality about George Meredith, for whom Wilde had a profound admiration, that he cried: "Oh, Meredith is a prose Browning", and then with a chuckle of delight at the good thing which he had just discovered—"and so's Browning".

His wit bubbled fresh from the source, and the suggestion of labour and the midnight lamp which the first half of the third act of *Lady Windermere's Fan* did convey was due to nothing more than that he was working rather uneasily in a medium to which he was not as yet accustomed. He felt crowded, he had not time enough, space enough for all the amusing quips and comments he wished to make. So he crammed them into an enclave too narrow. They were not too good, but too many to be true. Wilde made no such mistake when he wrote *The Importance of Being Earnest*. He was the master of his machine by then and he wrote that best of farces within a month.

It is impossible, however, to read the letters which during the rehearsals passed between the author and the manager—very feudal and lordly letters from Wilde and purely practical ones from Alexander—without realising that it was the manager at this time who was the more conscious of the two of the creaking conventions, the clever twists, the impossible transitions of character which were making the drama of the day a by-word; who was the more anxious of the two to discard them. The worn-out machinery was still rumbling, the fan in fact was still fluttering. At the end of the second act, as Wilde designed it, Mrs Erlynne was to tear off the stage in a tempest of words, the man to whom they were addressed was for the moment to cease to be, the audience was to be carried away by the acting of the leading lady. It was to be the conventional act-drop of a hundred sensational plays. Alexander, on the other hand, wanted the act to end not upon a tirade by the leading lady but upon a humorous and apposite comment by the man. The scene was to end on a stroke of comedy rather than on a blare of sensation.

The story of *Lady Windermere's Fan* needs here only the shortest summary. Lady Windermere, a beautiful prude of an extreme severity, believes that her mother died when she herself was a baby and idolises the old portrait of her which she possesses. But in fact Lady Windermere's mother bolted with a lover, and after twenty disordered years upon the Continent she is now, under the name of Mrs Erlynne, forcing her way back into society by blackmailing Lord Windermere with the truth of her identity. So long as he pays for her house and her parties, and secures her the invitations she wants, she'll hold her tongue. She has already a rather battered Lord Augustus Lorton seeking her hand. But a certain amount of scandal is awakened. Young Lord Windermere has taken a mistress and housed her in Curzon Street. So the gossip runs, and in due course reaches Lady Windermere's ears. She refuses to believe the gossip until on her own birthday ball Windermere sends a card to Mrs Erlynne and welcomes her to his mansion. Lady Windermere, like any other dramatic prude, flies off to the rooms of a courtier of her own, to pay her husband back in his own coin. But she leaves a letter of farewell for her husband. Mrs Erlynne discovers it, tears it open, reads it, realises that she is destroying her daughter's happiness, and in a revulsion of feeling dashes off to the courtier's rooms, to straighten things out if she can. This is the position at the end of the second act; and if the Importance of Mrs Erlynne's Secret is granted, the action of the play follows naturally.

LORD AUGUSTUS: Dear lady, I am in such suspense! May I not have an answer to my request?

MRS ERLYNNE: Lord Augustus, listen to me. You are to take Lord Windermere down to your club at once, and keep him there as long as possible. You understand?

LORD AUGUSTUS: But you said you wished me to keep early hours!

MRS ERLYNNE (*nervously*): Do what I tell you. Do what I tell you.

LORD AUGUSTUS: And my reward?

MRS ERLYNNE: Your reward? Your reward? Oh! ask me that to-morrow. But don't let Windermere out of your sight to-night. If you do I will never forgive you. I will never speak to you again. I'll have nothing to do with you. Remember you are to keep Windermere at your club, and don't let him come back to-night.

Act-Drop

Thus the play was written, but Alexander wanted another ending. Wilde wrote it reluctantly—an admirable little speech which completed the scene:

LORD AUGUSTUS: Well, really, I might be her husband already. Positively I might. (*Follows her in a bewildered manner.*)

Wilde having written the speech, retired to his bed at the Hotel Albemarle and fulminated in pencil:

With regard to the speech of Mrs Erlynne at the end of Act II, you must remember that until Wednesday night Mrs Erlynne rushed off the stage leaving Lord Augustus in a state of bewilderment. Such are the stage directions in the play. When the alteration in the business was made I don't know, but I should have been informed at once. It came on me with the shock of a surprise. I don't in any degree object to it. It is a different effect, that is all. It does not alter the psychological lines of the play. . . . To reproach me on Wednesday for not having written a speech for a situation on which I was not consulted and of which I was quite unaware was, of course, a wrong thing to do. With regard to the new speech written yesterday personally I think it adequate.

Alexander, however, was not inclined to accept the rebuke. He replied:

The end of the 2nd act is now better, but it could be better still and you could make it so if you took the trouble. I have pointed this out to you at almost every rehearsal but you only received my suggestion with contempt.

The change was made, and of course it was a small matter. The play was not endangered by either the presence or the absence of the two lines. But it is worth a moment's notice that it was the manager, the cockshy of the intellectuals, who stood out for the more natural and the more modern conclusion.

The second alteration was of a more vital importance. Wilde was anxious to keep altogether from the audience the knowledge that Mrs Erlynne was Lady Windermere's mother until the last act. To disclose the secret before, he writes,

would destroy the dramatic wonder excited by the incident of Mrs Erlynne taking the letter (*i.e.* the letter of Lady Windermere to her husband in which she abandons him) and opening it and sacrificing herself in the third act. If they knew Mrs Erlynne was the mother there would be no surprise in her sacrifice—it would be accepted. But in my play the sacrifice is dramatic and unexpected. The cry with which Mrs Erlynne flies into the other room on hearing Lord Augustus' voice, the wild pathetic cry of self-preservation, "Then it is I who am lost", would be repulsive from her, coming from the lips of one known to be the mother by the audience. It seems maternal and is dramatic coming from one who seems to be an adventuress, and who, while anxious to save Lady Windermere, thinks of her own safety when the crisis comes. Also it would destroy the last act; and the chief merit of my last act is to me the fact that it does not contain, as most plays do, the explanation of what the audience knows already, but that it is the sudden explanation of what the audience desired to know, followed immediately by the revelation of a character as yet untouched in literature.

Alexander nevertheless persisted. He was not likely to be persuaded into a discussion as to whether Mrs Erlynne was a character as yet untouched in literature. He was quite certain that to allow the audience to remain unaware of the reason of Lord Windermere's submission to the demands of Mrs Erlynne for the greater part of the play and then with a sharp twist to let them into the secret, would introduce a trickiness quite alien from and probably fatal to the success of the play. *Lady Windermere's Fan* would become a riddle long drawn out, instead of a play of real emotion and suspense.

I am perfectly certain, too [Alexander writes], that for the good of the play the audience should know very early in the second act, or at any rate at the end of it, that Mrs Erlynne is the mother—this too I have impressed upon you over and over again, but you have refused even to discuss it. The interest would be increased by this knowledge and Mrs

Erlynne and Lord Windermere would not be in a false position.

It was an old question. Should the audience be given the key to the play's problem, as Iago gives it in the tragedy of *Othello*, at the first possible moment? Should the interest to the audience lie in watching, itself freed from perplexity, the perplexed characters seeking the issue according to their natures and revealing their idiosyncrasies, their humours, their beliefs in the process? Or should the reason why of the play be held up until the last five minutes and disclosed to the audience and the personages on the stage in a *coup de théâtre* just before the final curtain is due to descend? Each spectator shall choose for himself and receive no blame whichever mode he prefers. But one is an appeal to the audience's ingenuity; the other to its pleasure in the development of character; or to put it in other words, the merit of the one lies in a puzzle, of the other in the telling of a story; and it is worth noting in any record of George Alexander that it was he who preferred the higher road of the story to the lower road of the acrostic.

Wilde in the end gave way. That Mrs Erlynne was Lady Windermere's mother was hinted at in the first act and disclosed in the second. Wilde rose from his bed and announced that he would return to the rehearsals.

With regard to matters personal between us, I trust that to-night will be quite harmonious and peaceful.

It was a pretty quarrel. Both author and manager were overworked and harassed. But it was a quarrel for which an enthusiastic reception on the first night and crowded houses afterwards provided a sufficiently alleviating balm; and in any case, as will be seen not once nor twice by any persistent reader of this history, quarrels between author and actor-manager, though they were less frequent, I think, at the St. James' Theatre than elsewhere, were still deeply planted in the natural order of things.

The Press was more divided than the public upon the attractiveness of the play. William Archer praised it with a rare warmth. Walkley was of the same opinion. Joseph Knight and his brethren scoffed; impervious people, they might have been born in Missouri, you had got to show them. Amongst the early visitors was H. D. Traill, an eminent man of letters who was the chief leader-writer of the *Daily Telegraph* under the editorship of the first Lord Burnham and an ardent playgoer. He wrote a longish letter to Alexander to which reference has already been made. He commented on the difficulty of the part of Lord Windermere; congratulated Alexander on his acting; argued that some less awkward way of bringing mother and daughter into collision might have been discovered; jested over the epigrams and continued:

On the other hand the dramatic quality of the whole play and the strength of the character-drawing seem to me considerable and not to have had justice done them. The play had to me the great attraction of increasing in interest throughout and the extremely rare merit of a strong fourth act. That I thought excellent in construction and the whole scene between you and Miss Marion Terry admirable and admirably acted. The cynical solution of the dramatic knot

on which the critics had so much to say is no more entirely
satisfactory than the sentimental one would have been.
Cynicism and sentiment divide life between them; if they
didn't you could predict human action much more often
than you can. Still it is refreshing to get the unmixedly
cynical solution for a change.

Wilde, to be sure, never looked upon his solution
as cynical at all. The second title of *Lady Windermere's Fan* is *A Play about a Good Woman*. But, I
think the truth is that even the intellectual playgoer
had grown so used to discovering in innumerable
last acts that the characters had been wrangling to
the point of tragedy over nothing more than a mistake, that he was baffled by a more genuine presentation of people and of knots which can never
be quite straightened out again.

> Yet bring into the silent gallery
> Some live thing to contrast in flesh and blood
> Some lion with the painted lion there
> You think she'll understand composedly?
> Not so!

The debate went on. There had been no play for
years so debated; with so much bitterness or with so
keen an admiration. There was still a trace of affecta-
tion no doubt, a clumsiness in the handling, a set
piece too publicly prepared. But the play was not
based upon an accident misunderstood. It dealt truly
with the primitive emotions, and these are the
foundations of literature throughout the world. A
new dramatist had come to town, however Joseph
and his brethren might dislike it. Old expedients
began to look uncommonly shabby. Alexander and

the St. James' Theatre and Wilde reaped their reward. The play ran through to the end of the year
(with the interval of a short tour) and made way
on December 3rd, 1892, for *Liberty Hall*, by R. C.
Carton.

§

That simple little comedy looks a trifle odd
wedged between the two high landmarks of *Lady
Windermere's Fan* and *The Second Mrs Tanqueray*.
R. C. Carton, the most modest of dramatists, was
the first to acknowledge that his play was on a
humble plane. He wrote to Alexander rather rue-
fully that he, a mere piece of earthenware, found
himself continually floating down the stream with
great iron pots in too close a proximity.

Modern criticism, rightly or wrongly, judges every new
piece not on its merits but in direct comparison with some
other or others and this is hard on earthenware.

Carton would not have lain under that disadvantage
to-day when, there being few theatres with permanent managements engaged in producing plays,
there are no immediate standards of comparison.
Nor could he have suffered at a date later than that
of this letter when he had written *Lord and Lady
Algy* and himself set a standard difficult to reach.
But the position which *Liberty Hall* occupied in the
order of Alexander's productions was a trifle un-
lucky for its author. It was a small modern fairy
story. Two girls, whose father had died, find the
estates entailed and themselves without a penny.
The heir is a young unknown cousin supposed to

be somewhere in the Himalayas. The heir appears disguised as a traveller in soap, and hands them a letter begging them to remain at the Hall until he returns. The elder sister's pride will not allow her to live there on sufferance. But there has been a mis-alliance in the family, and an old bookseller in Bloomsbury who is next door to bankruptcy offers the two girls a home on the strength of his distant relationship. In the parlour behind the shop, then, the characters gather for the rest of the play. The elder sister tries and fails to sell her amateurish paintings; Mr Owen, the supposed traveller in soap, occupies the second floor back; and Mr Todman, the book-seller, in spite of his excellent comedy lines, gets nearer and nearer to ruin. The young heir is, of course, the fairy godmother. He rescues Mr Todman from his oppression; he teaches the elder sister, who to tell the truth is a bit of a snob, that a girl, even with the traditions of "the Hall" at her back, may still find consolation in the love of a traveller in soap; and he saves the younger sister from being run away with by a young gentleman who has omitted the preliminary of a marriage certificate. It is a play, however, which can only be fairly judged when it is seen. It was meant to be acted. The lines were written to be spoken rather than read. It caught on. It ran for twenty-four weeks, earned on its London run more money than *Lady Windermere's Fan*, and two years later gained the *cachet* of Balmoral.

An extract from a letter written by Carton which refers to it may find a place here:

89 Ladbroke Road
Notting Hill Gate
Sunday

My dear Alexander,

The cheque reached me in perfect safety, and my pleasure at the *amount!* was not entirely selfish.

May I take this opportunity of giving my personal and written adhesion to the opinion of those who ascribe a *very large* proportion of our joint success to the perfection of the acting and the excellence of the "tout ensemble".

No dramatic author was ever more fortunate in his company—and *his manager!* One little word which I hope you will pardon. Many friends of yours and mine who have seen this play and are delighted with it—have hinted to me—that they thought some of the scenes were taken too slowly—and that most of the voices were pitched in too low a key. I mention this because I'm bound to say my own view of the matter is the same. I saw the first act on Thursday night and was impressed with the fact that *the first half* of it, especially, was taken too slow—and too low—! The first scene between the girls halted I thought. My wit (exquisite as some of the papers say it is) will not bear any lingering over.

I remember Irving once told me at rehearsal to be "confidential but loud"! This perhaps was not an altogether easy "stage direction", but you might urge them all (in the comedy scenes particularly) to be "*Idyllic*"—but *to hurry up!!!*

Once more forgive me. I am so happy and so proud about it all that it is rather a severe struggle to me to even hint at a qualification where all is so admirable. . . . In any case believe in the sincerity of my gratitude, and my regard!

Always yours,
R. C. Carton

I quote the letter for it shows that a fault about which complaints are loud to-day was as rife then; and it illustrates the relationship which used usually to exist between Alexander and the authors who wrote for his theatre. There was once an aged bookseller who said, "Nobody will meddle with authors: they create general apprehension and terror". Disputes there will certainly be, as there have always been, between authors and managers, and sometimes the disputes have been serious. I have never doubted that the turtle which smashed in the skull of Aeschylus was not dropped by an eagle at all but was hurled by the manager who was producing the *Agamemnon* after a more than usually acrimonious rehearsal. But the disputes at the St. James' Theatre, except in rare cases, ended with the conclusion of the rehearsals, and although Alexander's correspondence with authors was very large, I can find no trace that he was ever terrified by them or apprehended their approach. Whatever quarrels he had were composed without blood, and more often than not the quarrellers were shortly working together again at the St. James'. Alexander's letter-box, indeed, is full of such cordial phrases as those which Carton's letter contains. An author was an honoured person in King Street. His interference in the actual conduct of the rehearsals was welcome, at all events up to the moment when it became necessary to rehearse without interruption. His wishes were consulted over the cast and the scenery and the music to be played during the intervals between the acts. I remember that towards the end of the rehearsals of *The Witness for the Defence*, Alexander asked me, "How do you want the programme made out? That ought to be settled now." I was astonished, for the management had been in existence for twenty-one years and was likely to have its own methods. But Alexander answered, "No! We live here by agreeing with our authors". I preferred that the characters should be set down in the programme in the order of their entrance upon the stage as was commonly done in the French theatres; and that system was then, I think, for the first time adopted at the St. James'. A trifling matter, but from trifling matters things of moment may be inferred. The wind was tempered to the lamb and the lamb was not shorn.

Liberty Hall was produced in December 1892. But before that date *The Second Mrs Tanqueray* was in Alexander's hands and the title-rôle was being discussed. The play was intended for John Hare and the Garrick Theatre, but John Hare erred on the side of cautiousness. He found the play too daring and refused to produce it. Alexander quivered a little no doubt. *The Second Mrs Tanqueray* was the stark uncompromising tragedy of a woman whom the polite world was very willing to read about in novels but had only seen presented with the realism of the stage in the little theatres of the dramatic societies. In those corners, indeed, the New Drama, as its proud subscribers called it, might have remained, its fresh air still bottled for many years; until, indeed, the end of the war with its grand explosion of all restraints breached the walls of a million conventions. There was so much shouting in the corners, so much loud beating of little drums, that ordinary people were getting a little tired of it.

It needed more than a small amount of courage in the days when Shaw's *Mrs Warren's Profession* and Ibsen's *Ghosts* were forbidden audacities, for the manager of a theatre which drew its clients from the decorum of Mayfair and the respectability of the suburbs, to put up *The Second Mrs Tanqueray* even for a series of matinees. The "commercial" manager indeed who in his service to the art of the theatre still tried, the dreadful creature, to make both ends meet and indeed overlap at the end of the year—it was he who threw open the door. The Mrs Tanquerays up till now when they appeared upon the boards ended with pretty deaths in an atmosphere of tears and repentance and forgiveness. The public had wept too. It left its sense at home and brought only its sensibility to the stalls. It wept over its Frou-Frous and its Ladies of the Camellia and went back comfortably with the last words of "Cigarette" upon its lips: "So best". Pinero and the Company of the St. James' were to send it back if not uncomfortable, at all events a trifle exalted by the rare pleasure which comes from the spectacle of high achievement.

But so far the play has not been cast and only one name has been suggested for the poignant character of the Second Mrs Tanqueray.

"I can only say", Pinero wrote on October 28th, "that I hope we shall not be debarred from the privilege of soliciting Miss Nethersole's services."

Miss Olga Nethersole, who had not yet abandoned the stage to devote herself to social service in the East End of London, was Pinero's first choice, and again and again he came back to it. But she was under an engagement to John Hare, and it became more and more doubtful whether she could be secured. So by November 17th, Pinero was nursing another idea. He had seen Miss Janet Achurch play Nora in *The Doll's House* some years before at the Novelty Theatre and thought her a remarkable actress. Since then, however, she had toured in Australia, and that experience to his thinking had "accentuated certain vices of style". He added, "Certainly a few years ago she would have been the best Paula obtainable, and I had her in my mind for the part up to the time of her reappearance at the Avenue. . . . Perhaps we could do something with her if not for Paula, for Ellean!"

By December 21st, nearly three weeks after the first performance of *Liberty Hall*, Alexander was considering whether it would not be wise to delay the production of *The Second Mrs Tanqueray* until he could put it into the evening bill. He made the suggestion to Mrs Pinero quite informally at a party, giving as his reason that Miss Winifred Emery might then be available. Pinero's reaction to the suggestion, however, was not as favourable as one might have expected it to have been. He wanted his play produced, and though, as many and many a letter of his proves, he was the very last man to wish to shorten by a night the run of another man's play, he had in the arrangement for a series of matinees a more or less immediate opportunity which could do hurt to no one.

The great drawback to my mind is the delay it would occasion me in putting into evidence such work as I have been labouring at during the present year.

His heart was set upon the early production of his play. He was no doubt conscious that in depth and truth and emotional range it was on a higher plane than any work he had done before. It might not be so perfectly worded a piece of work as his hilarious farce *Dandy Dick*. But it aimed higher. If it was successful, he could not, in Carton's metaphor, fear collision with the biggest iron pot upon the stream. Here is a cry from the heart of any dramatic author:

The fittest time to begin rehearsing a play is, in my opinion, the day after it is finished.

On the other hand:

It strikes me, my dear Alexander, that in the enjoyment of your present success, and in the contemplation of the almost assured freedom from risk and anxiety for the rest of this season which this success gives you, you may feel *The Second Mrs Tanqueray* to be a little bit of an encumbrance. If you should entertain any such thought you will not, I hope, hesitate to express it. Should you even care to go so far as to discuss the advisability of entirely quashing our agreement, so that you may be relieved of what is now perhaps a burden and I given the freedom of trying my luck elsewhere, I will meet you, or see you here, at any time you appoint.

One of the dangers of waiting for Miss Emery is that one could get no absolute assurance that she would be able to act next season. Her health might be poor—a dozen chances might intervene.

Pardon this untidy scribble.

Yours sincerely,
ARTHUR W. PINERO

Alexander, however, was not unduly weighed

down by the burden. Nor did the possibility that Miss Winifred Emery might suddenly fall ill alarm him. So from Westgate-on-Sea, in the month of January 1893, Pinero is writing that he will be free early in Lent "to come to you and work on *The Second Mrs Tanqueray*". He has returned to his first choice for Paula.

Will Hare allow Miss Nethersole to act in your theatre in the morning while she is appearing in *Diplomacy* in the evening?

Alexander had proposed yet another actress in Miss Nethersole's place and the proposal seems to have tormented Pinero.

I do wish heartily I could bring myself to see her in the part but I writhe when I think of it. There are so many elements in Paula which would direct attention, I fear, to the indisputable maturity. I wish on your side you could imagine Mrs Beerbohm Tree as Ellean. This I fancy would be a good thing.

Alexander had in the course of these confabulations mooted the subject of incidental music, which was more commonly used then as an adjunct to emotion at the end of an act than it is now. The subject was dealt with briefly by Pinero and without enthusiasm:

As to incidental music, I can't see that anything of this sort is required. Don't you think "incidental" scraping vulgarises a piece that doesn't belong to either "the kettle-on-the-hob" or "the Blood-on-the-Breadknife" order of play? But of course I am open to any suggestion you are kind enough to make.

Pinero knew his own mind, but of course he was open to persuasion—in fact just as open as Sir

Anthony Absolute in Sheridan's comedy of *The Rivals*; and no more, so far as I can find, was heard of the incidental music.

By March 16th, 1893, it had been agreed between the author and the manager that *The Second Mrs Tanqueray*, instead of making the halting sort of appeal which a series of matinees would mean, should take its place for better or for worse in the evening bill as soon as *Liberty Hall* had run its course. The letter of Pinero which establishes this agreement contains two other items which deserve a place in any record of the St. James' Theatre. For one, Alexander was thinking of playing a version of *Rip Van Winkle*.

You would do wisely [Pinero replies], I believe, to follow the notion up. Get hold of the Boucicault play and the libretto of the more recent opera and compare them with Washington Irving's story. I will read these things too, if you like, and, should my engagements prevent me from actually doing the work for you, you shall at least have the benefit (!?) of my advice in the matter.

Nothing ever came of this notion, but it would have been interesting to have seen what the most advanced of the dramatic authors of the day would have made of that old legend. The second item was Alexander's decision to close his theatre and reply for the Royal General Theatrical Fund on the night when Pinero was to take the chair at the Annual Dinner. The decision was at once a tribute to the warm friendship which existed between the two men, and an act of more than common generosity. I suppose that we should call it a gesture nowadays, but since at the time when the decision was taken, *Liberty Hall* was playing to as much money as the old St. James' could hold, it was a little more practical than most of those we hear about.

Still the cast of *The Second Mrs Tanqueray* was as far as ever from being settled. One young lady was according to Pinero "a born understudy. You know what I mean. There was everything, words, actions, business, faithfully reproduced—everything but the feeling, the emotion of the character." This lady, therefore, did not play Ellean. Nor was he any longer thinking of Janet Achurch for Paula. "She is a little bit of a genius", but his confidence in her, never very strong, had faded altogether. There was Miss Hanbury—yes. "The best, the most attractive would be Miss Neilson." If Miss Emery would not bind herself for November—it looked at this date as though *Liberty Hall* would last the season out— they must put her out of their minds; and his hopes switched back to Olga Nethersole:

I don't think that Miss Nethersole will be in Hare's autumn bill unless he re-opens his theatre with a continuation of *Diplomacy*.

But there is just one sentence in this letter which points to the lady who in the end played the exacting part and in one night flashed to a leading place amongst the actresses of the world:

I will start my tour of the playhouses to-morrow night at the Adelphi.

For a year or two Herman Vezin had been touring the country with a repertoire of old plays and a young tragedienne and pupil in whose future he had unbounded faith. Arriving at a town of the Eastern Counties within reasonable reach of London, he had sought the presence of the London managers and critics at a matinee of Sheridan Knowles' play, *The Love Knot.* John Hare, one of the Gatti brothers, representatives of the Press, and others went down by train to the performance, and one and all came back with their mouths full of praise—not of the promised tragedienne, but of a quite unknown young actress who played the light comedy part, or a part of comedy as light as that turgid author could make it—a Mrs Patrick Campbell. In due course she was engaged for the Adelphi Theatre, where she appeared in a melodrama and strengthened the high opinion which had already been formed of her.

Four days after his earlier letter Pinero wrote again. Miss Maude Millett, whom Alexander had suggested for Ellean "held the field." As for Mrs Patrick Campbell, she was playing in such a poor piece that it was difficult to form an estimate of her powers. "She is, however, a very interesting actress, so much makes itself apparent." Pinero, however, found in her "a certain artificiality of style, engendered doubtless by her present situation and surroundings". Whether she could at the St. James' Theatre rid herself of it was a riddle which Pinero did not pretend to solve.

I should like you to see her [he wrote]; if you have another attack of influenza you might lie up in a box at the Adelphi.

Another two days, however, and it began to look as if another play would be required at the St. James'

before the season ended. *Liberty Hall* was fading
slowly out, and though not a character of the cast
had been definitely agreed upon, Pinero was eager
that *The Second Mrs Tanqueray* should no longer
be denied her opportunity. Leaving Paula out of
consideration for the moment he was quite satisfied
with the cast Alexander proposed, and as for Paula,
if neither Miss Neilson nor Mrs Campbell could be
secured, he was willing to consider whether the lady
of undeniable maturity could not be so reverently
and artistically restored as to revive a sense of
her original architectural proportions. "But Mrs
Patrick Campbell would be an interesting experiment."

Pinero was quite satisfied no doubt with the
names which Alexander suggested, but he was not
thereby debarred from criticising them and putting
forward others. Are you sure that Miss So-and-so
is really like Mrs Cortelyon? he asked. "Keep on
telling me she is, or I shall doubt it." In the end Amy
Roselle was engaged for that short but important
part. Cyril Maude was to all eyes the ideal Cayley
Drummle. Pinero wanted a ray of brightness—"in
a very serious play a ray of brightness is invaluable"
and a vein of sympathetic kindly geniality. But again
there was a large doubt whether Cyril Maude would
be free to accept an engagement at the St. James'.
Thereupon Pinero threw off a very interesting
speculation.

Hicks is a bright young actor. Would he look too much
like a young man with a wig on?

Seymour Hicks was twenty-three and looked

younger. His great talents as a comedian and his
irrepressible spirits had only lately lifted his head
above the wide flat waters of mediocrity. How would
his career have shaped if he had played the fine part
of Cayley Drummle in that notable production? But
Cayley Drummle must look his forty-five chirpy
years and Seymour Hicks went off to the Gaiety
and so to management on his own account. Pinero
wavered between Charles Allan, an actor with a
rasping voice long associated with the Haymarket
Theatre, and Brandon Thomas, the author of
Charley's Aunt. He inclined towards Brandon
Thomas, but Cyril Maude was at the last moment
available, and gave a polished and helpful rendering
of a character not too easy to represent. Meanwhile
Miss Elizabeth Robins was engaged to play Paula
Tanqueray. But at the last moment the Brothers
Gatti released Mrs Patrick Campbell, and Miss
Robins with the generosity of her high soul abdi-
cated what must have seemed to her the opportunity
of her life. It is pleasant to know that she took her
reward in another way and within a few years had
earned a serious reputation as a novelist of imagination and a subtle style. Ben Webster, a regular
member of the St. James' company, stepped naturally into the short but important part of Captain
Ardale and had lines as awkward to speak as any
that were ever written in a modern play. It was
always a mystery to me how any actor, however
skilful, even if half in and half out of a window,
could deliver such a speech as:

Isn't this fun? A rabbit ran across my foot while I was
hiding behind that old yew,

and reveal any sense of fun in delivering it. But Pinero is not the only playwright of great note who can make you feel hot-and-cold and shy as you sit in the stalls.

Amidst such obstacles and hindrances the play was cast. It was cast in the end as perfectly as human circumstance has ever allowed. It was acted by a company which was the best fitted in London to make clear and significant the tragic story which its author had to tell. But it needed months of negotiation, and suspense, and debate to get the company together; and that, too, at a time when theatres had a regular clientele and arrangements could be made ahead with a reasonable prospect of carrying them out. Those who are minded to condemn off-hand the more slovenly productions of our day may learn from this recital how enormous is the difficulty of securing the right cast under the happy-go-lucky conditions when a theatre must be snatched at the last moment and a cast assembled between dawn and dusk.

CHAPTER IV

The Second Mrs. Tanqueray · The vitality of the
play · Alexander's acting · His sincerity · Clement
Scott's charge of plagiarism · *Guy Domville*, by
Henry James

THE SECOND MRS. TANQUERAY is too well known a play
to need either analysis or description. Since it took
the playgoing world by storm over forty years ago
it has been revived so often that few playgoers can
have missed it; and the text of the play has been re-
printed sixteen times. It is a tragedy of relentless
logic from a text uttered by Paula Tanqueray herself
just before she kills herself: "I believe the future
is only the past again entered through another
gate". Accidental things—the sudden return of the
daughter, Ellean, from her convent, the unexpected
appearance of Captain Ardale—co-operate so to
twist the knot that only Paula's death can loosen it.
But the spectator is left with the conviction that any
other accidental things would have led to the same
end. For the cause, nay the end itself, lies in the
undisciplined character of Paula Tanqueray, a
character hardened beyond all reshaping in the
mould of her past passions. She has grown out
of the life she knew—she can no longer endure
the drunken Orreyd and his vulgar little doll of
a wife, but she is at home in no other life. She
is set in a purgatory of her own, jealous, dissatisfied, a creature of wild moods, mean acts, bitter

56

regrets, and every now and then a fine and generous impulse.

Incidents in the play may seem to us now anti-quated and over-stressed. Should we take as so serious a breach of good manners Ardale's visit to say good-night to his lady-love? It is true that he trespasses, that he has not been formally introduced, that he slips through a hedge and crosses a meadow which belongs to his prospective father-in-law. But would the loved one herself be so annoyed, so severely reproach him? Would the father-in-law-to-be take so austere a view of Captain Ardale's eager-ness? It might even be held that the relationship in which Paula Tanqueray, Ellean, and Captain Ardale stood to one another—that is, Captain Ardale be-trothed to the step-daughter of the woman with whom he has lived—would be regarded with less horror to-day. But it may be, on the other hand, that it is the fashion of our times which is evanescent and that a later day may bring back a rigid code, where all these proprieties will seem once more natural and just.

The Graduate
Mrs Robinson

Character, however, does not date. The char-acters of Paula and of Aubrey Tanqueray, the lonely man who deludes himself that he can build up a life of happiness upon such a marriage, belong to all the ages; and the author who can set these people out in the garb which they wore and the manner in which they lived and the code which they obeyed in any era, may, for all we know, belong to all the ages too. Great authors when their work is over seem to follow a divine rule in that they perish for a while and come to life again and then only take their seats in the

chairs of Fame. Defoe and Tennyson and Trollope
are to be found now in that Hall. Shakespeare for
many years after his death was held of small account.
Meredith awaits the verdict of Time. There were
two playwrights, Wilde and Pinero, whose best
work was acted by Alexander at the St. James'
Theatre; and both of them reflected more than the
passing shadows of their day. If I dwell overmuch,
in this record of an actor's career, on the work those
authors did, I have Alexander's warrant for it. Actor
and author were not to be dissociated. At the invitation of Will Crooks he made a speech at Poplar on
the encouragement of play-going as a rational form
of amusement and instruction; and in the course of
it he declared:

It is true that the writer of the play is the more important
factor, for without him the actor's work is of little avail.

And a little later on in his speech he added:

Literary men and actors have always been closely associated with each other; for they have been able to help each
other.

Certainly Alexander helped no less as actor than
producer. The care which he lavished upon his plays
has obscured to some degree his merits as an actor.
But they were great. Some of the chief parts which
he played, Rassendyll, Karl Heinrich, Aubrey Tanqueray, have been played since by actors of high
reputation, but they have never been given the same
authority. The plays themselves have suffered from
his absence rather more than from the lapse of time.
One can still remember the moment in the first act
of *The Second Mrs Tanqueray* when he read the

letter from his daughter which announced that she had abandoned the religious life and was returning to his side. The second Mrs Tanqueray-to-be was in the room.

"What are you staring at?" she asked. "Don't you admire my cloak?"

"Yes", Aubrey answered. But all the trouble which was to come and the grim end to it were mirrored in his face. And in the final scene he acted with so quiet a tenderness, so hopeless a patience that one's heart ached for his misery. Even those who did not like the play and were exhorting him to put before his public "good wholesome dramas which would elevate the rising generation", paid their tribute to his mastery of his art. Letter after letter written to him immediately after the performance tells of people in a quiver of emotion. Alexander had made his way as an actor before he became a manager. He believed in and respected the art of acting; and in consequence he brought to every part that he played an intense sincerity, a determination to extract from it and show all that it had to show. There was never a private joke carried on upon the stage of the St. James' Theatre to the ruin of the play and the decline of the actors who indulged in it. Could anything be more destructive of an evening's enjoyment than to be aware that a jest to which the audience has not the secret is occupying the attention of the company, instead of the play which it is supposed to be acting? Half-stifled laughter, grimaces made in a vain effort to keep a face serious, whispers under the breath— who has not lost an evening through some such tedious and insolent exhibition and decided to do without that particular theatre for the future? Alexander took pride and with justice in nothing more than in the sincerity of his acting. At a later period, half-way through the war, the dramatic critic of the *Evening Standard and St. James' Gazette* took violent exception to Alexander's revival of *Bella Donna*. The revival was "a practical satire upon the way in which we mismanage our English theatre"—whatever that phrase may mean. Following an unfortunate precedent of the late Lord Salisbury this critic called an Egyptian nobleman a "black" man, and suggested that Alexander in the part of Dr. Isaacson disguised himself as though he were loth to be too closely identified with it.

The attack was ferocious, coming at a time when the difficulties of keeping open a theatre not devoted to revues or the detection of spies were growing with every week. It took Alexander on the raw, and he protested. An interesting correspondence followed. The critic said that at this time one had no energy for controversy outside one's work for the war. So if Sir George Alexander told him that the war had for the time being shelved all the standards, he would retire altogether from an impossible position. Alexander agreed that one had no energy for controversy outside one's war work—as a matter of fact what with his work on the Collections Committee of the Red Cross, his organisation of matinees, and his efforts for the League of Mercy, he was exhausting a constitution already undermined and driving himself steadily to his death. He did not impugn the critic's honesty and he claimed as much honesty for himself.

"But I think your statements that we mismanage our English theatre and that 'Sir George Alexander disguises himself for the part as though he were loth to be too closely identified with it, are assertions which are unfair and should not be allowed to pass without protest."

The critic replied that the word "mismanaged" was not directed against the St. James' Theatre and he admitted that a critic had no right to suggest even by implication that an actor had not an absolute faith in his part. From Alexander's point of view nothing less than an act of treachery had been imputed to him. He would no more have played a part of which he was ashamed, or in which he did not believe, than he would have tried to make another actor laugh when they were both acting a serious scene. He was a fine comedy actor, he could point an epigram or get all the fun out of farce, but he must not be thought to be playing the fool. He was the very serious practitioner of an executive art. Authors may not be good prophets of their own work. A number of happy and confident letters written on the eve of a complete failure bear pathetic witness to it. But they can be excellent judges of the truth and competence with which their characters have been portrayed. And the letters written in a humbler vein after the failures express whole-heartedly enough their thanks for the ability of the acting. "I am to blame" was the common message to the St. James' on the morning after a defeat; and after a success, a reasoned tribute testified not only to the good relations between the manager and the author, but to the excellence of Alexander's acting. Here is one

from the well-known man of letters, W. L. Courtney, written from the office of the *Daily Telegraph* on the night of the production of his one-act play *Kit Marlowe*.

Daily Telegraph
FLEET STREET, LONDON, E.C.
Oct. 31

MY DEAR ALEXANDER,

    I cannot do my work to-night without sending you a line about your impersonation of "Kit". I could not say it to you personally—for I can not "heave my heart into my mouth", any more than Cordelia could. But no author could possibly dream of a better hero than you made mine. In all sincerity you were just the ideal poet whom I was trying to describe—with the happiest changes from grave to gay, from comedy to tragedy, and through it all just that touch of impending doom, which is of the essence of romance. It came to me as a revelation—not of your powers, for I knew them before—but of my own dream.

    How I longed for you to appear on the scene!, for the sketch was hanging fire a bit till your vitality gave it life.

    I do not know, nor do I care much, what the critics may say of my play, except for your sake. But I do not envy the man who could see you unmoved, or fail to feel what a truly poetic atmosphere you lifted us into.

Ever yours gratefully,
W. L. COURTNEY

It is amusing, by the way, to notice in how many instances the critic turned dramatist disdains the opinions of his brethren and expects their blame.

I could fill fifty pages with praise as enthusiastic and grateful from other authors upon their several occasions.

§

The Second Mrs Tanqueray, on its initial run, was played two hundred and twenty-seven times in London, and the money paid to see it amounted to £36,688 : 13s. It is to be remembered that this was before the house was remodelled and its seating capacity enlarged. The run was broken for ten weeks by a provincial tour. Alexander, following the example of his great chief, Henry Irving, had been steadily working up, by successive tours, a close connection with the playgoers of the great provincial towns. During this autumn of 1893 he visited eight of them and the suburban theatre of Islington. Alexander included four plays in his repertoire, *The Second Mrs Tanqueray*, *Liberty Hall*, *Lady Windermere's Fan*, and *The Idler*. His share of the receipts during the ten weeks amounted to £7300 : 10 : 3, and of that amount £4392 : 9 : 8 was taken by *The Second Mrs Tanqueray*. The play roused a great deal of discussion in its progress, and at Birmingham especially a newspaper controversy broke out. *Lady Windermere's Fan* and *The Idler* had both been seen upon the tour of the previous year. *The Second Mrs Tanqueray* was the new bill and occupied the stage for the greater number of evenings.

It was not, however, only the audacity of the play which provoked attack. Clement Scott, the dramatic critic of the *Daily Telegraph*, launched in the *Illustrated London News* a definite charge of plagiarism against its author. He declared that Pinero had taken much more than his subject from a German play, *Der Schatten*, written by Lindau. Pinero's reply was a writ for libel. He put the case into the hands of Sir George Lewis, regretting that the times had gone by when a public caning would have been the permitted way to meet the charge. The article appeared half-way through August. Yet towards the end of September, Clement Scott is writing to Pinero, "People are making mischief between us—we are such old friends too! I wish to do everything that an honourable man ought to do." Pinero sent this piece of wheedling on unanswered to Sir George Lewis, who demanded from Clement Scott a with-drawal of the charge and a formal and explicit apology. A letter accordingly was drawn up by Sir George, and in his presence and in that of Pinero Clement Scott signed it. And there, one might have thought, the matter would have ended.

But Clement Scott's apology was one of the pen, not of the mind. A few years later he revived his charge, but now in the *Morning Telegraph* of New York. In New York he couldn't be touched by the law of England. He could slander as he willed; and he seized the occasion of another startling dramatic coincidence, as he termed it in inverted commas, to repeat his attack. In the *Morning Telegraph* of September 10th, 1900, he wrote:

The Second Mrs Tanqueray was produced at the St. James' by Alexander. It was then found to be an echo of Lindau's *Der Schatten*, adapted by the American critic Meltzer, who had previously read it to an English actress of some repute. Another dramatic coincidence. They are all speaking the truth. I believe Pinero. . . . In fact, I believe everybody—but is there a ghost walking about the St. James' Theatre who tells plots to destitute dramatists?

The malice in the paragraph is evident and it is to be welcomed. For it revealed that the aim was rather to wound than to repair an injustice. To class an author of Pinero's output and invention amongst the dramatists destitute of plots was an illuminating piece of folly. The paragraph, moreover, brought the lie direct from the American critic Meltzer. He wrote to Sir George Alexander from New York on September 14th, 1900:

MY DEAR SIR,

My attention has just been called to certain statements attributed to Mr Clement Scott by the New York *Morning Telegraph*. I have written to Mr Scott, denying that I ever made an adaptation of Lindau's *Der Schatten* or submitted one to an English actress, and begging him to contradict his mistaken assertion.

At the time of the first production in America of *The Second Mrs Tanqueray* I published a signed review of the play in the New York *World* in which I suggested that Pinero's admirable work and Lindau's had *both* been inspired by some foreign drama—possibly Portuguese or Spanish.

Believe me,
My dear Sir,
Very faithfully yours,
CHARLES HENRY MELTZER
Formerly dramatic critic of the New York
Herald and New York *World*.

George Alexander, Esq.

But why should Meltzer make the suggestion that both Pinero and Lindau had been inspired by an unknown foreign dramatist? The subject of the play is not so rare that it needs a microscope to discover it, and once that subject is chosen by two men living in the same age and both of them playwrights, points of likeness are certain to appear. To my mind, it is astonishing that many more cases of similarity do not occur. They do at times, of course. There is an author living in London to-day who, having just finished his play, saw its replica presented, and put his own away in a drawer: where it remains. It seems, too, as if from time to time a subject gets into the air and is breathed in by more than one. It is not two years ago since two plays upon the Brontë family were produced within a few days of one another. Two plays with Nell Gwynne as the heroine ran side by side, one at the Haymarket with Julia Neilson playing the orange-girl, the other at the Prince of Wales' with Marie Tempest. When one counts up all the plays which are written and submitted, the miracle is not that here and there two deal with the same theme but that so few challenge any comparison at all. There is certainly no reason to assume that an author in Germany and an author in England both found the same obscure play in a foreign language, and set to work to transcribe it as their own. But there is and always will be a class of jealous persons who, when they are forced to discover that a fine thing is fine, cannot bring themselves to acknowledge that the man they know who did it, did it out of his own genius and wits.

§

The Second Mrs Tanqueray ended its long run on April 21st, 1894, and a week later *The Masqueraders*, a strong romantic play by Henry Arthur Jones, took its place. Both Alexander and Mrs Patrick Campbell were again together in the principal parts, and gained an immediate success. Pinero, who found it a torment to see his own plays acted, could take the keenest and most generous enjoyment in the plays of his fellow dramatists. After being present on the night of July 25, he wrote:

> 63 HAMILTON TERRACE, N.W.
> 26th July 1894
>
> MY DEAR ALEC,
> I had no opportunity last night, without running the risk of appearing to be merely complimentary, of telling you that I thought your acting of David Remon strong, sympathetic, and altogether delightful. No part that you have played, in my recollection, has brought out the grace and tenderness of your method so effectively.
> As for the play, I could see it again to-night with the utmost pleasure: I don't often get this feeling nowadays.
>
> Yours always,
> P.

The Masqueraders ran until the August holidays, shared the bill with *The Second Mrs Tanqueray* on the subsequent tour, and returned to see the year out at the St. James' Theatre.

There followed upon January 5th of 1895 one of those experiments which made Alexander's management so honourable an affair. The play which he produced was a financial failure, chiefly indeed owing to the costly elegance in which it was framed and set; and it received on its opening performance an unmannerly and derisive greeting from the cheaper parts of the house.

Henry James was a cultured American who had long made his home in England. He lived a sheltered, smooth life in a pleasant circle of friends. He wrote some exquisite and some very forcible short stories; but for the most part he wrote with infinite care uneventful novels which reflected faithfully the milder scenes of those well-mannered Victorian days. He had a small, select, and rather idolatrous public of his own; fans in fact. A. B. Walkley, for instance, the ingenious dramatic critic of *The Times*, once told me that he read the whole of Henry James once a year. James was, in addition, a man of means, and he divided his time between London and Rye, where he had a beautiful house panelled in mahogany and as polished as himself. It should be added that the moment the war broke upon England he got himself made a British citizen so that he might share the dangers and embarrassments of that country whose hospitality he had so long enjoyed. He was very particular and fastidious in his tastes. There was a touch of the old maid in him, and a precision in his speech which led him to add clause upon clause and qualification upon qualification, to express the exact shade of his meaning. He made a noble profession of faith when he renounced his American citizenship, and being now eligible for the coveted Order of Merit, was awarded it. A life of contentment no doubt, but there were crumpled rose-leaves even in his bed. He would have liked to have ridden a horse, so that he might live more intimately the English life of the countryside. He would have liked to have climbed mountains, believing that so he would have captured and been able to express that elusive passion for the hills which baffles the most skilful pens. In fact he was like nine people out of ten. He wanted to do the things which nature and the habit of his life had told him to leave to others. But I think that above all things, and again like nine people out of ten, he wanted to write a successful play.

He had tried his hand already. For he had dramatised his own novel *The American* for Edward Compton, and that well-known exponent of the eighteenth-century comedies had produced it, during one of his London seasons, at the old Opera Comique in the Strand. It was almost inevitable then that the actor-manager who was actively trying to discover new playwrights and Henry James should be drawn into some sort of concatenation. The two men met. Henry James had three subjects in his mind: a three-act contemporary comedy, a three-act contemporary play, "less purely a comedy but on a subject very beautiful to my sense", and *Guy Domville*, a play set in the eighteenth century. Unfortunately it was *Guy Domville* which was preferred by both men, and Henry James retired to Wellington Crescent, Ramsgate, to get on with the work. The script of the first act was sent, scenarios of the last two followed. Alexander was asked to remember that James was fully aware "of the lacunae which real treatment of the subject must make good (and will); all the transitions it will smooth over, all the insufficiently explained things it will vivify, all the expression and colour, all the lucidity and atmosphere, and superiority I shall undertake to make it supply". So what with remembering all these things and acting at night, Alexander must have had a pretty busy time of it.

Henry James then took his courage in both hands

to mention in advance—he seems in their conversations to have kept this little matter slyly up his sleeve—that "his *dénouement* does not belong to the class of ending conventionally termed happy".

Mrs Tanqueray [he writes] seems to me to have performed the very valuable service of showing that the poor dear old British public, in whose name such imbecilities are committed, can rise to a denouement that isn't a mere daub of rose-colour.

Henry in fact was up on his toes.

Terms were arranged, the play completed and rehearsed with an admirable company which included, besides Alexander himself, H. V. Esmond, Herbert Waring, W. G. Elliott, Marion Terry, Irene Vanbrugh, and Evelyn Millard. And on Saturday, January 5th, of 1895, the first performance was given. But alas, the poor dear old British public rose to the *dénouement* in a quite unexpected way. When the curtain fell, there were vociferous cries of "Author! author!" Behind the scenes the call was misunderstood. Somehow a blunder was made. The curtain was raised again and Alexander led on Henry James to such an explosion of cat-calls and boos and hisses as was seldom heard even in those days when first-night disturbances were not uncommon. H. G. Wells was present as the dramatic critic of the *Pall Mall Gazette* and he has given in the second volume of his Autobiography a vivid description of the scene.

It was too much for Henry James. He was not the man for violence and brawls. He was too sensitive, too thin-skinned. He took his reception much more seriously than there was any need to do. I remember

reading a published letter which he wrote long afterwards to his brother. The recollection of that sea
of hostile faces white against the dark background of
the gallery, still oppressed him as something horrible
and vile. He wrote no more for the stage.

CHAPTER V

AT the St. James' Theatre clearly something had
to be done and quickly. *Guy Domville* was certainly
playing to an average of £90 a performance, but
the receipts were dropping. There were plays enough
in the making but none made. This management
had been in existence only for four years and the
time was not yet ripe for revivals. The young manager
was in a quandary. But as it happened, in the early
summer of the previous year Wilde had conceived
the idea of a farcical comedy, and some correspondence had taken place between himself and Alexander
about it. Wilde, however, was uncertain about the
proper theatre for the piece. It seemed to him more
suitable to Charles Wyndham or Charles Hawtrey
than to George Alexander. Alexander moreover was
seriously considering a visit to the United States,
and if he were to produce the comedy in London,
he would want it for his tour in America. But such
a plan was outside Wilde's reckonings altogether.
He wrote frankly to Alexander that John Palmer,
at one time a famous American impresario, wanted
a comedy from him "with no real serious interest".

As regards the American rights, when you go to the States it won't be to produce a farcical comedy. You will go as a romantic actor of modern and costume pieces. My play, though the dialogue is sheer comedy, and the best I have ever written, is of course in idea farcical. It could not be made part of a repertoire of serious or classical pieces—except for fun—once—as Irving plays Jeremy Diddler to show the Bostonians how versatile he is and how a man who can realise Hamlet for us, can yet hold his own with the best of fantastic farce players.

I would be charmed to write a modern comedy-drama for you—and to give you rights on both sides of the disappointing Atlantic Ocean—but you, of all our young actors, should not go to America to play farcical comedy—you might just as well star at Philadelphia in *Dr. Bill.*

Besides I hope to make at least £3000 in the States with this play—so what sum could I ask you for with reference to double rights? Something that you, as a sensible manager, would not dream of paying. No: I want to come back to you —I would like to have my play done by you (I must tell you candidly that the two young men's parts are equally good) but it would be neither for your artistic reputation as a star in the States, nor for my pecuniary advantage, for you to produce it for a couple of nights in each big American town. It would be throwing the thing away. I may mention that the play is an admirable play. I can't come up to town; I have no money.

Wilde at this time, the summer of 1894, was terribly pressed for money. "I am sorry my life is so marred and maimed by extravagance", he wrote on another occasion to Alexander. "But I cannot live otherwise. I, at any rate, pay the penalty of suffering." But Wilde was an artist. He could shut out his duns on the doorstep of his mind and dwell within amongst the lively creatures of his fancy; and if whilst he worked he heard from time to time the knocking of those duns, it merely quickened his pen. Thus in a single month of 1894, at Worthing, he wrote *The Importance of Being Earnest*.

Before the farce was written, but when it had taken shape in his thoughts, he sent a short description of it to Alexander:

The real charm of the play, if it is to have a charm, must be in the dialogue. The plot is slight but, I think, adequate. ... Well, I think an amusing thing with lots of fun and wit might be made. If you think so too, and care to have the refusal of it—do let me know—and send me £150. If when the play is finished, you think it too slight—not serious enough—of course you can have the £150 back. I want to go away and write it—and it could be ready in October, as I have nothing else to do. . . . In the meanwhile, my dear Aleck, I am so pressed for money that I don't know what to do. Of course I am extravagant—you have always been a good wise friend to me—so think what you can do.

More than one groundless attack has been made upon Alexander for his dealings with Wilde and this chapter will have to take them up. Meanwhile, Wilde's own words should be borne in mind. Alexander had always been a good wise friend to that ill-starred man and he was to prove so to the end of Wilde's life.

In the autumn the play was finished. Wilde had a bout of fever, and from his bed wrote to Alexander again:

As you wished to see my somewhat farcical comedy, I send you the first copy of it. It is called "Lady Lancing" on the cover: but the real title is *The Importance of Being Earnest*. When you read the play you will see the punning title's meaning. Of course the play is not suitable to you at all. You are a romantic actor: the people in it want actors like Wyndham and Hawtrey. Also you would be sorry if you altered the definite artistic line of progress you have always followed at the St. James's. But, of course—read it and let me know what you think about it. I have very good offers from America for it.

Of what happened immediately thereafter there is no evidence. Either Alexander thought the play too slight or Wilde thought the actor too serious, and by Christmas of that year, 1894, *The Importance of Being Earnest* was in the hands of Charles Wyndham. The failure of *Guy Domville*, however, made Alexander ask for it. Wyndham was in no immediate need of a play and he agreed to concede it on the condition that Alexander should consent to Wilde's "writing me an original play before he writes yours".

Alexander on his side, consented. He wrote on February 7th, 1895:

MY DEAR WYNDHAM,

If Wilde is desirous of doing your play first I will not stand in the way—my scenario, of course, not being touched.

You had better, therefore, make your arrangements with Wilde himself.

Sincerely yours,

G. A.

From this arrangement it is apparent that there was a second play by Wilde, or rather the scenario of a second play, in existence upon which Alexander had a claim; and that the writing of this second play was to be deferred until Wilde had written a third play for Charles Wyndham. It is necessary to be clear upon this matter, for a question of literary honesty is involved. There *was* a second play mapped out, of which the scenario was in Alexander's possession. The scenario will be produced later on in this chapter; and it will be seen that although Wilde never wrote it, it was written. It appeared over another name, was produced at another theatre, and because of the strength of its theme it had some success, even though there was none of Oscar Wilde's wit to embellish it. For the moment, however, I am concerned only with *The Importance of Being Earnest*.

It was put into rehearsal as soon as it became evident that *Guy Domville* could not be hoped long to survive his catastrophic debut. Alexander as usual was at the pains to assemble the best cast which he could obtain. For the part "equal to his own"—that of Algernon Moncrieffe—he secured an admirable comedian in Allan Aynesworth, who was to appear in nine other productions at the St. James' Theatre. Miss Rose Leclercq was the Lady Bracknell who had a passion for cucumber sandwiches and thought that to be born or at any rate bred in a handbag, whether it had handles or not, displayed a contempt for the ordinary decencies of family life that reminded her of the worst excesses of the French Revolution. The two girls were played by Irene Vanbrugh and Evelyn Millard, who a year later was by her beauty and charm to make still more famous Anthony Hope's Princess Flavia. Miss Prism and Canon Chasuble found their exact representatives in H. H. Vincent and Mrs George Canninge, whilst the two

menservants fell to Franklin Dyall and Kinsey
Peile. A small cast but one upon which it would have
been difficult to have improved.

"I know that you are at one with me", Mrs Pearl
Craigie wrote to Alexander in July of 1898 with
reference to her own one-act play *A Repentance*, "in
thinking that an actor of genius has everything to
gain and nothing to lose by having the best talent
possible among his supporters—and particularly in
the case of those with whom he has scenes. The
Irving method of frittering away priceless vitality
on dead-weights has proved but too dangerous. The
stronger the cast, the clearer the triumph."

Here Mrs Craigie was a little unfair to Sir Henry
Irving. Irving surrounded himself habitually with
the most efficient actors. One has only to remember
his matchless production of *Much Ado About Nothing*
to be sure of it. But he cut down the parts they
played, so that their importance was diminished, and
spectators familiar with a play of many good characters would be aware of only one of them and might
well fancy that the others were insignificantly played.
At the St. James', however, the play was the thing.

The rehearsals, however, in the case of *The Importance of Being Earnest*, dragged a little in spite of
the excellent company. Wilde himself was fractious.
His interruptions were so continuous that no scene
could be taken through from the beginning to the
end; and the day appointed for the production was
coming near. Alexander accordingly took him aside
and said:

"We know now everything you want and if
you'll leave us alone to get on with the rehearsals we

shall try our best to give it to you. But if you don't, we shall never be ready. So I'll send you a box for the first night and see you again after the performance."

According to Alexander's story, Wilde was for a moment taken aback. But then with tremendous solemnity he replied:

"My dear Aleck, I have still one more thing to say to you and to Aynesworth. So if you will both of you come and have supper with me to-night at the Albemarle Club, I shall not trouble you again."

It sounded portentous and alarming. Both Alexander and Aynesworth, tired with a long evening's rehearsal, walked up St. James' Street a little anxious and worried. What further alteration could Wilde want at this time of day? Of what did he now complain? They were met in the hall of the club by Wilde in full evening dress. He laid one friendly hand on Alexander's shoulder, the other upon Aynesworth's.

"My dear Aleck," he said, "and my dear Tony. I have only one thing to say to you. You are neither of you my favourite actor. We will now go in to supper."

He then left the company to its own efforts and was interviewed the day before the production by a reporter who asked him whether he thought the play would be a success.

"My dear fellow," Wilde expostulated, "you have got it wrong. The play *is* a success. The only question is whether the first night's audience will be one."

The first night's audience turned out to be a brilliant success. The delicious absurdity of the opening dialogue between Jack Worthing and Algernon Moncrieffe, Worthing's love-scene with Gwendolen, his story of his origin, Lady Bracknell's indignation,

GEORGE ALEXANDER
AS WORTHING IN *THE IMPORTANCE OF BEING EARNEST*

and Algy's intention to impersonate to Worthing's pretty ward in the country Worthing's quite imaginary wicked brother, kept the audience in delight until the curtain fell upon the first act; and in suspense until it rose upon the second. Perhaps the culminating moment of the farce—for a glorified farce is what it is—was when Worthing with a face of woe, dressed to his hat-band and his gloves and his pocket-handkerchief in the deepest mourning for the immoral brother who had died in Paris, paced on to the stage ignorant of what the audience knew; that the immoral brother in the person of Algernon Moncrieffe was actually within the house, making love to his ward. Alexander never acted with a lighter or more confident touch; he was well matched with Allan Aynesworth, a brilliant comedian with that power to sound a deeper emotion without which comedy is second-rate; the ladies were fair to look upon and had caught the fantastic spirit of the piece; and if, to use the American language, *Guy Domville* had been a flop, *The Importance of Being Earnest* was an indubitable wow.

When Wilde went round from his box to the long room, at the side of which Alexander dressed, Alexander said to him: "Well, wasn't I right? What did you think of it?"

Wilde, his large face smiling, nodded his head in the odd, ponderous way of his and answered: "My dear Aleck, it was charming, quite charming. And, do you know, from time to time I was reminded of a play I once wrote myself, called *The Importance of Being Earnest.*"

The farce thus started upon what looked to be a

golden career, but as everyone knows, a horrid
disaster came with the summer. In 1902 it was revived for fifty-five nights and returned a slight profit.
But it was not until the winter of 1909 that it received full recognition. Time had softened judgment, the work the man did was no longer to be
obscured by the man's faults. *The Importance of
Being Earnest* ran for eleven months and remains
alive amongst the few great farces which can survive
the passing of the epoch in which they were written.

§

In the second volume of his *Life of Oscar Wilde*
Frank Harris attacks Alexander on the ground that
just before Wilde's trial he took Wilde's name off
the bill as the author of the comedy. Harris con-
trasts Alexander's conduct with that of Charles
Wyndham. He makes Charles Wyndham say that
if a play of Wilde's was put on at his theatre, the
author's name must be on all bills and placards as
usual. He would not allow his theatre to be used to
insult a man upon his trial. All this sounds very
heroic, and it is certain that Wilde's name was taken
off the bills of *The Importance of Being Earnest* and
was retained on those of *An Ideal Husband*. But
Alexander was better aware of the financial distress
in which Wilde was labouring. The essential thing
for him was money and again money—not money
to pay old bills, but money for his immediate needs.
The English public was more hypocritical in the
last years of the nineteenth century than it is to-day.
Alexander counted upon that hypocrisy. It seemed
to him possible that with Wilde's name off the bills

the life of the play might be prolonged. Given time, it might even outsail the storm of vituperation and anger and hatred. If it did, there would be royalties to fill Wilde's empty purse. In the event the plan failed. Not merely did justifiable indignation flame high, but every petty jealousy and rancour, all that there was of uncharitableness and ill-will brought out its little set of bellows to blow the flame still higher. There could be no mention of the man's name, no discussion of his work. On the music-halls every red-nosed comedian made his little cheap joke to yells of laughter. *The Importance of Being Earnest* foundered, and it may be that Alexander made a mistake in taking Wilde's name off the bills. He certainly did no good to himself. But to this extent he was justified. *The Importance of Being Earnest* was able to hold the stage for a month longer than *An Ideal Husband.* There were a month's more royalties for the author. The last night of *An Ideal Husband* was April 13th; that of *The Importance of Being Earnest,* May 10th.

Frank Harris puts the complaint into the mouth of Wilde himself with other assertions which are open to flat disproof. There are pages and pages of a conversation between Harris and Wilde, which is supposed to have taken place in 1898, that is, eighteen years before the *Life* was published. The conversations are in inverted commas, the supposed actual words which were spoken. I-said-to-him-and-he-said-to-me stories, whether told or written, are always untrue. When told, they are even more intolerably tedious than untrue. For you see them being made up in front of you, and they are pointless, and you cannot escape without some explosion of ill-manners. You are held by the narrator's eye, even as the ancient mariner held one of three. It is related that the late Lord Birkenhead, being detained in some such bondage in his club, rang for the waiter and said to that astonished man, "Will you please hear the rest of this story for me? I haven't the time." Most of us weaker vessels have not that courage. We sit, shifting in our chairs, the prisoners of tedium and disbelief. A good story is trim and neat and makes his bow smartly and has done with it. But the I-said-to-him kind is a sloven among stories and the teller of it is Public Enemy No. 1. When, however, those stories are written down, they may not be so tedious—for you can skip them—but they are infinitely more false. Long conversations, word by word, cannot be remembered for eighteen years. The author's own predilections colour them. What he wants to be said slips in as having been said. The author's thoughts, even his imaginings, are attributed to the other partner in the dialogue. They are uttered with a greater authority that way. Thus Wilde is represented as saying:

I was sitting by the roadside on the way to Cannes. I had taken out a Vergil with me and had begun reading it. As I sat there reading, I happened to raise my eyes, and who should I see but George Alexander—George Alexander on a bicycle. I had known him intimately in the old days, and naturally I got up delighted to see him, and went towards him. But he turned his head aside and pedalled past me deliberately. He meant to cut me. . . . Think of Alexander, who made all his money out of my works, cutting me, Alexander! It is too ignoble. Wouldn't you be angry, Frank?

It is very possible that this bitter speech was never made at all. On the other hand, the gentlest man will, under a grievance, mistaken or true, utter an injustice—and hope that his biographer will not print it in his book afterwards. But these words have been printed and so they must be examined. Let us take first of all the phrase "Alexander, who made all his money out of my works". An additional reason for doubting that these words were ever spoken, or if spoken, were spoken seriously, is that Wilde knew and must have known that they were untrue.

Here are the facts. The date of this diffuse conversation is a day towards the end of the year 1898. Up to that time, the net profits (that is, after the author's royalties, the cost of the dresses and the scenery, the salaries of the actors, actresses, and those concerned in the business management, and the weekly cost of the theatre, had been discharged) from *Lady Windermere's Fan* amounted to:

On the London run, Feb. 20th to July 29th, 1892	£5712	0	6
On the tour from August 22nd to October 29th	451	13	4
	£6163	13	10
Less the loss on the revival in London from Oct. 31st-Nov. 30th, 1892 . . .	717	16	6
	£5445	17	4
Lady Windermere's Fan shared the bill on the tour of 1893 with *The Second Mrs Tanqueray*, *Liberty Hall*, and *The Idler*, and its share of the net profit amounted to .	124	3	7
	£5570	0	11

The play was not revived again until the autumn of 1904. So that at this time, the winter of 1898, £5570 : 0 : 11 had been made by Alexander out of Wilde's works.

From this sum, however, must be deducted the loss on the first run of *The Importance of Being Earnest*—it was not until the year 1909–1910 that the comedy made its triumphant success—and this amounted to £289 : 8 : 4.

The net result is that Alexander had made, at the time when Wilde is described as making this statement, out of Wilde's works, exactly:

$$£5570 \quad 0 \quad 11$$
$$289 \quad 8 \quad 4$$

$$£5280 \quad 12 \quad 7$$

But Alexander had then been in management for eight years and the net profits of those eight years, as audited by his accountants, apart altogether from Wilde's works, came to:

Dr. Bill	£3,669	19	10
The Idler	2,699	1	8
Liberty Hall	6,498	9	3
The Second Mrs Tanqueray . . .	10,946	5	2
The Masqueraders	5,679	17	11
The Prisoner of Zenda . . .	10,483	17	9
As You Like It	1,020	6	5
The Tree of Knowledge . . .	3,559	4	0
The Ambassador	4,255	3	0
Tours	12,486	17	9

£61,299 2 9

This total leaves out the money lost upon failures. All that is required here is the proportion which the profits on Wilde's works bore to the sum of the profits upon the other plays. And it is clear from these figures that anyone claiming that Wilde was at this date responsible for Alexander's financial success would be talking the sheerest nonsense.

The speech attributed to Wilde, however, contains a grave charge. It states that Alexander bicycling on a road which passed Napoule in the South of France cut Wilde dead. The simplest answer is to print the following letter written two years afterwards:

July 1900
HOTEL D'ALSACE
RUE DES BEAUX (ARTS?) PARIS

MY DEAR ALECK,

It was really a great pleasure to see you again and to receive your friendly grasp of the hand after so many years, nor shall I forget your dear wife's charming and affectionate greeting of me. I know now the value of things like that.

With regard to your proposal to spread the payment for the plays over a certain time, I know it was dictated by sheer kindness and the thoughtfulness of an old friend. If you would send Robert Ross £20 on the first of every month for me it would be a great boon. He would send it on to me as he looks after all my affairs. His address is R. B. Ross, 24 Hornton St., Kensington, W. I would then have before me a year free from worry, and perhaps may do something you would like.

Could you do this for me?

I was very delighted to see you so well and so unchanged. Kindest wishes to your wife,

Sincerely,

OSCAR WILDE

It is incredible that if Alexander and his wife were greeting Wilde in Paris with so much friendliness in the summer of 1900, Alexander bicycling alone on a country road in the South of France, eighteen months before, should have cut him dead. There is too great an inconsistency. If there were any basis for the story at all, it might be that either Wilde mistook his bicyclist or Alexander did not see Wilde. But it may well have been manufactured. Frank Harris was not very scrupulous whether the blow was fair, so long as the blow was dealt. Wilde's own letter must hold the field. There is, besides, heaps of evidence to show that all the way to the end of his life Alexander was the "good wise friend" of Wilde's earlier letter. He bought the acting rights of *Lady Windermere's Fan* and *The Importance of Being Earnest* when Wilde went bankrupt; he had got a bargain and might have stood upon his rights as many another man in similar cases has. But he did not whilst he lived. And when he died he bequeathed the rights he held to Oscar Wilde's son.

§

Earlier in this chapter mention has been made of a scenario, for which a sum in advance of the royalties on the completed play had been paid by Alexander. Here is the scenario. It will be seen that it is addressed from Worthing, and therefore cannot be of a date later than the summer of 1894. For Wilde did not go back there. It was written out in fact whilst Wilde was working upon *The Importance of Being Earnest*.

THE HAVEN
5 ESPLANADE, WORTHING

DEAR ALECK,

What do you think of this for a play for you? A man of rank and fashion marries a simple sweet country girl—a lady—but simple and ignorant of fashionable life. They live at his country place and after a time he gets bored with her, and invites down a lot of fashionable *fin-de-siècle* women and men; the play opens by his lecturing his wife how to behave —not to be prudish, etc.—and not to mind if anyone flirts with her—he says to her, "I have asked Gerald Lancing who used to admire you so much—flirt with him as much as you like".

The guests arrive, they are horrid to the wife—they think her dowdy and dull. The husband flirts with Lady X. Gerald is nice and sweet and friendly to the wife.

Act II.—The same evening—after dinner—Love scene between the husband and Lady X: they agree to meet in the drawing-room after everyone has retired. The guests bid good-night to the wife. The wife is tired and falls half asleep on a sofa. Enter husband: *he lowers the lamps:* then Lady X arrives—*he locks the door*. Love scene between them—wife hears it all. Suddenly violent beating on the door. Voice of Lady X's husband outside—desiring admittance. Terror of Lady X! Wife rises, turns up the lamp and goes to the door and unlocks it—Lady X's husband enters! Wife says "I am afraid I have kept Lady X up too late; we were trying an absurd experiment in thought reading" (anything will do). Lady X retires with her husband. Wife then left alone with her own husband. He comes towards her. She says "Don't touch me". He retires.

Then enter Gerald—says he has been alarmed by noises —thought there were robbers—wife tells him everything— he is full of indignation, it is evident he loves the wife. She goes to her room.

Act III.—Gerald's rooms—wife comes to see him—it is clear that they love each other. They settle to go away together—enter servant with card! The husband has called. No one is frightened, but Gerald consents to see him. Wife retires into another room.

Husband is rather repentant. He implores Gerald to use his influence with the wife to make her forgive him. (Husband is a gross sentimental materialist.) Gerald promises that he will do so—it is evident that it is a great act of self sacrifice for him—exit husband with maudlin expressions of gratitude.

Enter wife: Gerald asks her to go back to her husband. She refuses with scorn—he says, "You know what it costs me to ask you to do that. Do not you see that I am really sacrificing myself?" Etc. She considers: "Why should you sacrifice me?—I love you. You have made me love you—you have no right to hand my life over to anyone else. All this self sacrifice is wrong, we are meant to live. That is the meaning of life." Etc. She forces him by her appeals and her beauty and her love to take her away with him.

Three months afterwards: Act IV.—Gerald and wife together—she is reading Act IV of *Frou-Frou*—they talk about it. A duel between Gerald and the husband is fixed for the day on which the scene takes place—she is confident he will not be killed—he goes out. Husband enters. Wife proclaims her love for her lover—nothing would induce her to go back to her husband—of the two she wishes him to die. "Why?" says husband. "Because the father of my child must live." Husband goes out—pistols are heard—he has killed himself.

Enter Gerald, the husband not having appeared at the duel. "What a coward", says Gerald. "No", she answers, "not at the end—he is dead." "We must love one another devotedly now." Curtain falls with Gerald and the wife clinging to each other as if with a mad desire to make love eternal—*Finis*.

What do you think of this idea?

I think it extremely strong. *I want the sheer passion of love to dominate everything*. No morbid self sacrifice. No renunciation—a sheer flame of love between a man and a woman. That is what the play is to rise to—from the social chatter of Act I, through the theatrical effectiveness of Act II, up to the psychology with its great *dénouement* in Act III, till love dominates Act IV and accepts the death of the husband as in a way its proper right—leaving love its tragedy—and so making it a still greater passion.

Of course I have only scribbled this off—I only thought of the plot this morning—but I send it to you—I see great things in it—and, if you like it when done, you can have it for America.

Yours,
Oscar

In his Life of Oscar Wilde, Frank Harris gives another of his conversations with that author. He speaks of a scene which Wilde described to him, calling it a great stage picture. It is spoken of again as "a screen scene", and in the scenario above it is the scene in the second act where the wife unlocks the door. Frank Harris continues:

That evening thinking over what he had said, I realised all at once that a story I had in mind to write would suit "the screen scene" of Oscar's scenario; why shouldn't I write a play instead of a story? When we met next day I broached the idea to Oscar:

"I have a story in my head", I said, "which would fit into that scenario of yours, so far as you have sketched it to me. I could write it as a play and do the second, third, and fourth acts very quickly, as all the personages are alive to me. Could you do the first act?"

The idea of the collaboration was a mistake; but it seemed to me at the moment the best way to get him to do something. Suddenly he asked me to give him £50 for the scenario at once, then I could do what I liked with it.

After a good deal of talk I consented to give him the £50 if he would promise to write the first act; he promised and I gave him the money.

It appears from this narrative that all that the play was to owe to Wilde was the first act in which this scene presumably was to have been incorporated. But that story won't do. Mrs Patrick Campbell produced Frank Harris' play of *Mr and Mrs Daventry* at the Royalty Theatre on October 25th, 1900. It not only had the screen scene in just the same position as it occupied in Wilde's letter to Alexander, but the rest of his scenario too, the same characters, the same *dénouement*. No doubt the play would have been a totally different thing if Wilde had written it. But the story and the characters which made it live were Wilde's from the beginning to the end. Frank Harris adds an appendix to his book which does not succeed in diminishing his debt and does not make any greater acknowledgment of it. He is not to be trusted.

§

Years afterwards, on May 10th, 1914, Alexander revived *An Ideal Husband*. But the last act of that play was never satisfactory. According to Wilde's executor Robert Ross, John Hare refused the play on that account. There were too many exits and entrances, and there was a certain fussiness when the comedy should be moving quite definitely and certainly to its end. It ran only to July 27th and lost nearly two thousand pounds. Ross was anxious that Alexander should produce a translation of Wilde's play of *Salomé* and persuade the Censor to lift the ban upon it. In one form or another *Salomé* was performed regularly in the United States and in all the countries of Europe except England. But Alexander was not attracted to the subject and Ross' plan came to nothing.

Salomé was written in French by Wilde, who wrote the language with a classic accuracy but spoke it with an atrocious accent. There is extant a well-authenticated anecdote which may close this chapter. On the occasion of a dinner given in Paris, Émile Zola was to propose the toast of "The Arts" and Oscar Wilde was to reply. Zola spoke, of course, in French, and in coupling the toast with Wilde's name, said, "Malheureusement Mr Wilde sera obligé de répondre dans sa langue barbare".

Wilde began his reply in French too. He said, "Je suis Irlandais de naissance, Anglais de race, et comme le dit M. Zola, condamné à parler la langue de Shakespeare!"

CHAPTER VI

1895 a black year · Henry Arthur Jones · *The Triumph of the Philistines* · Alexander's domestic life · Offer by Andros de la Rue to back a production of *Hamlet* · Anthony Hope Hawkins · *The Prisoner of Zenda* · Great success of the play · A comparison of receipts

WITH the collapse of *The Importance of Being Earnest*, once more in that year, 1895, something had to be done, and quickly. Henry Arthur Jones, who had scored one success at the St. James' with *The Masqueraders*, had now another play ready called *The Triumph of the Philistines*; at the moment an unfortunate title. It was produced on May 11th, the night after *The Importance of Being Earnest* was withdrawn. Henry Arthur Jones was the stormy petrel of the stage. With the appearance and the diction, and indeed the past of a commercial traveller, he had been endowed with a passion for culture and he had educated himself chiefly upon the great poets and the prose writings of Matthew Arnold. He was a man of large ideas violently expressed. Critics like Bernard Shaw and Max Beerbohm expected his work with eagerness and criticised it with care. Most of the others were repelled by an uncouthness in his style and the untempered vigour of his convictions. He was the most positive man you could meet in a twelvemonth. Causes were tonics to him and he drank of them greedily. The question of the censorship of plays provoked speeches and letters and a pamphlet of forty-six pages. Furious with a system which allowed the actor-manager to dominate the rehearsals and print his name bigger than the author's, he took the old Avenue Theatre, the home of *Dr. Bill*, and put on his own play *The Crusaders*, just to show how things should be done. He staged it beautifully with Morris tapestries and a rose-garden which I remember still as one of the loveliest scenes I ever saw, and had a complete failure. The venture cost him £4000, as his daughter relates in her Life of him, and £4000 lost upon a single play in a small theatre meant in those days a heavy loss indeed. But Henry Arthur Jones had the resilience of a boy, and dropping the iniquities of the actor-manager, he turned his enthusiasms upon the Shakespeare Memorial Theatre. When he had done with that, there was still the great battle over Free Trade and Protection; and towards the end of his life he felt that a public duty was laid upon him to annihilate Bernard Shaw. "That man will be the death of me", he said when he was lunching at the Dramatists' Club. But in fact that man kept him alive, for he had never learned to idle comfortably. The pamphleteering of Henry Arthur Jones was too rhetorical to annihilate anyone. Reading it one seemed to be listening to a front-bench speech in a Victorian Parliament. What point it had was blunted by his verbosity. There were invocations, there was satire, but the invocations were lost upon the air, and the satire was not sharp enough to hurt. But he had the reward of indomitable old warriors. He kept the good-will of those whom he attacked, and everybody whom he knew liked him well. The courage of his views and his indomitability he carried into his private life. For he suffered at the hands of surgeons the severest of the major operations, and survived them all. He was as tough as rubber and came back like rubber. He was generous in his praise, kind to the beginners in his craft, and the most copious letter-writer of his generation. He wrote ninety-one plays besides, of which *The Liars* and *Mrs Dane's Defence* are probably the most famous; and the plays, like himself, were, as a rule, neither mellifluous nor small.

It can be inferred from this short sketch that Henry Arthur Jones was not a restful element in a theatre. A friend with whom he was lunching at the Garrick Club during the rehearsals of *Carnac Sahib* at His Majesty's Theatre asked him, "And how are you getting on this time with Beerbohm Tree?" Jones answered heartily, "Oh, very well indeed! I had to send him my solicitor this morning, otherwise things are smooth!" and the stories were rife of the times when he leaped across the orchestra and stumped out of a theatre, and when he was barred out of the rehearsals of his plays. The following letter, accordingly, written towards the end of the run of *The Masqueraders* in 1894, bears a valuable testimony to the tact with which the St. James' Theatre was conducted.

TOWNSHEND HOUSE
NORTH GATE, REGENT'S PARK
Thursday, July 19/94

MY DEAR ALEC,

Many thanks for your kind gift of the photograph and many more for the inscription on it.

I have never had so pleasant an association with any

theatre as I have lately had with yours. Long may it continue.

Always yours,
HENRY ARTHUR JONES

Henry Arthur Jones wrote three plays for Alexander, of which only the first, *The Masqueraders*,
had any success. The *Triumph of the Philistines* began
as a satire upon the self-righteousness of the British
public and ended by becoming too self-righteous
itself. He took a village in the Midlands, the home of
a shoemaking industry, and invented for its inhabitants such a group of Puritanical rogues as
even the most violent of preachers would hesitate to
collect together for a series of sermons. Here they
were all crowded together in one. The hypocritical
Little-Bethelite has been an easy mark for centuries
and more. The man who discovered him deserves
half the fees of half the authors in the world.
Molière made play with him; Dickens used him;
every author of an historical novel set in the days of
Cromwell has made a target of him; but no playwright put him into so many shapes, and so crudely
bedaubed those shapes, and so weighed them with
their own false weights, as did Henry Arthur Jones
in *The Triumph of the Philistines*. He was supposed
to know the middle-class tradesmen of the provinces
and very likely he did, but in this play he let his
dislike of them run away with him. Even their
names were a caricature—Jorgan, Pote, Blagg,
Modlin, Wapes, Skewett. They hadn't a chance, had
they? On the other hand, the brilliant young artist
was called Willie Hesselwood and the hero Sir
Valentine Fellowes! So heavy-handed a satire could

hardly do anything but sting you into revolt against
its author. The most mercenary of harlots brought,
of course, the chief and most oppressive Puritan to the
ground—a French harlot too. Yes, she was French
and she spoke with a broken accent and she had
not one grace or allurement except those which Miss
Juliette Nesville could give her; and M. Augustin
Filon of the *Revue des Deux Mondes* said that her
author had penetrated into the *état d'âme* of another
nation! Alexander himself played Sir Valentine
Fellowes and the part made no demand upon him
and offered him no opportunity. As always, the cast
was of the highest efficiency. Actors of the worth of
Herbert Waring, H. V. Esmond, E. M. Robson,
Ernest Hendrie, James Welch, and actresses like
Lady Monckton and Miss Nesville could do nothing
to save a play which fell so far below the high
standard of its author. The play had forty performances, cost Alexander a smallish sum, and was
replaced by a revival of *The Second Mrs Tanqueray*.
But that great play was restored to the bill too soon,
and for the last week of the season it gave way to
The Idler.

A tour of ten weeks produced a profit of some
four hundred pounds less than either of the two
previous tours. But the tour had a compensation.
Alexander and his company were commanded to
Balmoral, and on September 17th they played
Liberty Hall in the presence of Queen Victoria and
her Court. A Royal Command was a rare honour,
and to a young manager of not yet five years' standing it meant prestige at the moment and material
benefit in the future. For Alexander was gradually

gathering a regular band of theatre-goers at his theatre, people who must see the new play at the St. James' whatever the newspapers said about it; people from the big houses in the suburbs as well as the artists, doctors, judges, and dwellers in inner London who filled the stalls and the dress-circle during the first performances. The Balmoral Command was bound to increase in a very solid fashion the number of his patrons. Alexander reopened the St. James' Theatre on November 7th and the short autumn season did not help. *Liberty Hall* was revived for a fortnight, and then twenty performances exhausted the new comedy by H. V. Esmond, *The Divided Way*. Claude Carton, writing to Alexander on November 26th of that year three days after the first night of this play, summarised the general view: "If there is a doubt expressed here and there as to the play—everyone unites in giving the highest possible praise to your individual share in it". *The Divided Way* was withdrawn on December 14th and the theatre was closed. Thus the blackest year which the young management had passed through came to an end. Four new plays had been produced, and three old successes revived, and every one of them had lost money. To make matters worse, at the height of the mischance, during the run of *The Triumph of the Philistines*, the Alexanders fulfilling an arrangement made months before, moved from their small house in Park Row to one a good deal more spacious and costly in Pont Street.

The set-back would have been more serious but for the prudence with which the theatre was administered. Alexander had had his warning when his

manager bolted with the profits of *Dr. Bill.* There
was no parsimony in the conduct of the business but
all the care proper to a great undertaking in which
from its very nature heavy losses must from time to
time occur. What was wanted was paid for and got,
but without extravagance. There were producers of
plays in those days and, for all I know, there may
be now, who would buy the rarest old carpets from
Turkestan to cover the floor of a corridor which was
seen two or three times for a second when a door was
opened. But no such follies were committed at the
St. James' Theatre. He paid high salaries, after a discussion, for he wanted the characters in his plays to
be well acted; he paid high royalties, for he wanted
the best plays on the market; and he practised a
careful and reasonable economy, for he wanted his
management to continue. He whipped a play off
quickly when the receipts fell—it was said, sometimes too quickly. But when a play failed the loss
amounted to the least possible sum, often little more
than the cost of the scenery and the dresses; and both
scenery and dresses went into store for future use.
The losses on these four productions and three
revivals, set out in detail, ran thus:

The Importance of Being Earnest . .	£289	8 4
Guy Domville	1873	7 2
The Triumph of the Philistines . .	803	10 3
The Divided Way	897	17 0
The Second Mrs Tanqueray (revived) .	655	1 2
The Idler (revived) . . .	421	7 0
Liberty Hall (revived) . . .	392	12 3
A total of . .	£5333	3 2

Brought forward £5333	3	2

But on the other hand, the profit on the tour
amounted to   1901   14   11

And so reduced his loss to .   .   £3431   8   3

But even this sum does not represent
actual loss. For he was down on his
books as a salaried actor at £80 a
week. He drew for instance as a
salary during the run of

Guy Domville . . .	£283 6 8		
The Triumph of the Philistines	416 13 4		
The Divided Way . .	183 6 8		
The Importance of Being			
Earnest . . .	640 0 0	1523	6 8

£1908   1   7

A few small items alter this sum. He lost £97 on a
company touring *The Triumph of the Philistines* and
he made £35 : 15 : 2 in the same way from *Guy
Domville*. So the actual loss upon the twelvemonth's
work amounted to a sum a little short of £1900. But
he had thrown into the scales a year's hard work.

It was a distressing experience for anyone, and for
a man of moods a serious discouragement. Alexander
like most rather shy, reticent, and sensitive men had
armoured himself with a mask of indifference. He
seemed to some difficult of approach, aloof. It was all
armour. He was within the armour a man of an intense
sensibility. He was in the clouds one moment, in the
lowest caverns of gloom the next. Were there empty
benches in the Upper Circle and the Pit, at once he

cried, "The cheaper parts are the backbone of the theatre". If the returns warned him to reduce the number of the stalls and widen the spaces between the tiers, at once he argued, "At the St. James', we live upon our stalls. Unless they are full, we must move into a third floor back."

He was blessed, however, in that he had throughout his life a devoted wife at his side. Lady Alexander took a very notable part in such practical matters as the dresses and the decoration of the stage. But the aid and sustainment she brought to him in their private lives were tremendous factors in the success of his management. When he was at his moodiest, she was at her cheerful best. It was not that she pretended that a failure was a triumph. That would have been of no use. Figures are figures, and Alexander had been trained to value them at their due worth. But when he began to contemplate his calamities under a magnifying-glass, she took the magnifying-glass out of his hands, and showed them to be just such rebuffs and misadventures as it is the common lot of striving men to encounter. He was indeed sufficiently enheartened to contemplate during this disastrous autumn a production of *Hamlet*. He was ambitious as an actor; he was still young enough to look the part; his long experience at the Lyceum had given him a freedom in the clothes of an older period than his own which few actors possessed; and if his voice was no cathedral organ it had as much range and flexibility as others which had been heard in that part. On the other hand, the stage of the theatre had to be reckoned with. This was the year 1895 and the St. James' was not remodelled until 1900. Was there depth enough not merely for the changes of scene but for the dignity of the tragedy itself? He had accustomed his audiences to expect his plays in an appropriate environment. They looked for "the confederate season and all things agreeing". *Hamlet* made puny would have cancelled a portion of his good-will. Alexander talked of his project amongst his friends and—I call it one of the consolations of that year—one morning came a letter from an old friend, T. Andros de la Rue, then Mr Andros de la Rue. He was made a baronet in 1898 and died in 1911. His letter encouraged Alexander to be "on the move", and backed the encouragement in the most practical form:

I am doubtful whether "St. James's" holds money enough for it to be a financial success here. In America you will doubtless coin money over it. I shall be delighted to lend you three thousand pounds without interest to be repaid just *when* and how you like. Let me know when you are likely to want the money—I suppose early next year.

This very year with its tragedy and its losses must have confirmed Alexander's knowledge that he had chosen in Mr MacDougall's words a profession which was precarious as well as laborious. A production of *Hamlet* at his own cost must have made a serious inroad into his savings, and if unsuccessful, have hampered his activities in the immediate future. Mr de la Rue's offer, therefore, was of a singularly persuasive kind. But just at this time a play came to his hand which, if it was to be produced at all, ought to be produced at once.

Anthony Hope Hawkins, after a distinguished

career at Oxford—he was an Exhibitioner of Balliol, became President of the Union, and took a First in Greats—was admitted to the Bar, and during the early nineties was devilling in the chambers of H. H. Asquith, the Prime Minister to be. There was no young man then living of whom a great legal career could have been more confidently prophesied. He was an eloquent and witty speaker; he had a beautiful voice, a very exact knowledge of what he knew, and a great charm of manner. His curious deep gurgling laugh made him your friend, above all if it was what you said that provoked the laugh. In politics he was a keen and sensible Liberal. It seemed, taking it all in all, that the way to high office in the House of Commons would be straight for him and not too difficult. He had already in 1893 a practice in railway work, and at the General Election of 1892 he had contested the Tory stronghold of South Bucks. Meanwhile he had in his spare hours been writing fiction, treating large subjects with a light and urbane touch. Four novels had been published, and although none of them had been definitely successful, they were recognised as heralds of success. In November of the year 1893—he tells the story in his *Memories and Notes*—as he walked from the Westminster County Court, where he had conducted and won a case, back to the Temple, the story of *The Prisoner of Zenda* came into his mind. The book was written off at white heat, sometimes a chapter in the morning and another chapter at night. It was finished before the year was out. Immediately afterwards he wrote a series of sketches in dialogue which during the spring of 1894 appeared in the *Westminster Gazette*.

GEORGE ALEXANDER AND ANTHONY HOPE HAWKINS

The Dolly Dialogues and *The Prisoner of Zenda* were published within a few weeks of one another, *The Prisoner of Zenda* in April; and between them they swept the reading public off its feet. Anthony Hawkins had now to make his choice. If he were to continue at the Bar and share out his life between legal work and politics, he must shut the door on Anthony Hope. He might drive a tandem, he couldn't drive a Roman chariot. He couldn't be, like Mrs Malaprop's Cerberus, three gentlemen in one. He decided to be Anthony Hope. In after years I think that he regretted his choice, but there were more early primroses on the path of literature. He abandoned his practice in the Law Courts and, taking a couple of rooms in Buckingham Street, Strand, close to the Watergate, as a workshop, he sat down to write.

I did not know him until three years later, but he quickly became one of my greatest friends and remained so until his death. He was the pleasantest of companions, sane in his judgments, witty in his talk, kindly but with just enough formalin in the milk to keep it sound, and altogether too diffident about himself. He added a word to the English language, and that is more than most novelists can claim.

The Prisoner of Zenda was dramatised for him by Edward Rose, one of Anthony's many friends amongst the actors. Rose had adapted already Anstey Guthrie's *Vice-Versa* with a certain amount of efficiency. But his version of Anthony Hope's romance excited little expectation amongst the managers of theatres. The play went the round. There was a quite justified disinclination to present adaptations of novels; partly through the fault of the adaptors, and still more because the novel is a leisurely affair and much more akin to the film with the film's facility for transition than it is to the play. When a novel is transferred to the stage, what is required is rather a transmutation than an adaptation. It has to be stripped to its skeleton, and then built up again in its new shape. To transfer wedges of dialogue, to compress scenes which were written to be read, to select incidents which happened in different places and force them to happen in one, to thin out characters which have become famous through their elaboration, so that they may at all events bear their names and wear their clothes before an audience, is to fall between two stools. And this is what usually happens. The quality of the book is lost, and a poor thing with ragged edges vainly pretends that it is a play. *The Prisoner of Zenda*, therefore, went round and round. It tarried for a while in the hands of Forbes-Robertson. But in 1895 it was produced in New York by Edward Sothern, who held in America a position parallel to that which Alexander held in England. To what extent it was altered during the course of the rehearsals I have no knowledge. But with the parts of Rudolf Rassendyll and Rudolph the Fifth, King of Ruritania, acted by the greatest romantic actor in America, the play took the New York public by storm. It was no longer negligible in England. Alexander sent an emissary across the Atlantic to see it, secured it, and on January 7th, 1896, produced it at the St. James' Theatre.

He had always a remarkable flair for the actress

who was standing on the threshold of theatrical fame, and waiting for just the right cue to make a startling entrance. On this occasion Alexander spoke it to Evelyn Millard, whose beauty and appealing tenderness were undoubtedly of the greatest value to the play. Alexander himself at that time was superlatively fitted to play the dual rôle. He could be romantic in modern clothes, and romantic in costume, and in this play he had to be both. His good-looks, his appearance, his humour and high spirits gave at once the impression of a youth who goes into a high adventure for a lark. And the change to a man called upon to fight not only against his living corporeal enemies, but against all the temptations of passion for the salvation of his soul, was made with an emotional restraint which was true and sure. He won the whole-hearted admiration of his public and the praise most valued by an artist of those who worked in the same field. Pinero, as acute and wakeful a judge as could be found, generous with his applause when it was deserved but unhesitating in his censure when it was not, wrote:

We had a delightful evening in witnessing *The Prisoner of Zenda*. It is a charming piece and most brilliantly put upon the stage. You and I must talk much about it when we meet: I watched everything with great care and am full of appreciation of the excellent work of actors and authors. I don't think you, as an actor, have been seen to greater advantage in any play you have produced. I compliment Mrs Alexander, too, upon the ladies' dresses. They are most beautiful.

And from the host of Alexander's friends congratulations poured in. The character of Princess Flavia was no less dramatic than that of Rudolf Rassendyll. To use the modern jargon, they were neither of them static. Her awakening to the change in the King who courted her; her surprise, her suspicion; the political betrothal transmuted magically into love; her renunciation when at last she knew the truth— all these elements built up a character which was inevitably sympathetic, if presented with sincerity and charm. Evelyn Millard had both those qualities and was well matched with Alexander. The adventuress and mistress of Michael, Duke of Strelsau, the Black Elphberg, Antoinette de Mauban, was played by Lily Hanbury who had been borrowed from Beerbohm Tree. Herbert Waring was the Black Elphberg, W. H. Vernon the Colonel Sapt, Allan Aynesworth the young English artist, Bertram Bertrand, Arthur Royston the Fritz von Tarlenheim, whilst the very important part of Rupert of Hentzau, "the boy who came so nigh to beating me", as Rassendyll describes him in the book, was filled by Laurence Cautley.

It is worth while here to print two letters written to Alexander by the adaptor Edward Rose. For they illustrate the relationship which remained firm between Alexander and the authors whose plays he produced, after the strain and the squabbles of rehearsals. The play had its *première* on a Thursday evening, and the first letter was written on the Sunday preceding it:

Sun: 5 *Jan:* 96
My dear Alexander,   36 Upper Addison Gardens, W.
    I am not very good at saying things, but I must try to tell you how very deeply I feel the way in which you have

given yourself to this production of *The Prisoner*. I have never seen anything like the unselfishness, and the care and patience, and the constant intelligence of your stage-management; and your manner has made the most trying rehearsals a pleasure—it has been so easy to suggest anything, and everyone must have felt that his or her interests, however small, had the fullest consideration. I am only glad to think that this sort of thing repays itself in the result; and very very glad to believe that—whatever is the fate of the play—you will yourself make the greatest personal success you have ever had.

I felt this so strongly that I had to write, now that my share of the work is over. I shall come round to see to-morrow's rehearsal, but *not* to interrupt. Now I'll make my final suggestion: comedy, comedy, comedy wherever possible!

I got a hint from the Wilson Barrett play. I think the moon might quite legitimately have travelled a little way round the heavens during Act 4—so that from Hentzau's exit its light is falling on the place where Flavia will finally stand, and we shall end with a beautiful picture of the girl's white figure. Don't you think so?

Do *start* the rehearsal with Acts 3 and 4, and go through them with the object of getting speed all round, while you are fresh; then walk the rest!

Thank you a thousand times!

EDWARD ROSE

The second letter was written on the morning following the production:

36 UPPER ADDISON GARDENS, W.
Wed: 8 Jan: 96

MY DEAR ALEXANDER,

My first letter on this beautiful desk must be written to you—not only to thank you for it (as I did most imperfectly in the midst of the tumults last night) but to thank you once again, and not for the first time nor the last, for all that it commemorates. What that is, you can't know because you can never see what I saw last night—a presentation of my play I think as delightful and complete as any author ever saw of his own work. It was an added and a very great pleasure to find that the climax of the play *at last* gave you your chance—and to see how you seized it, and how the audience leaped at it!

Ever yours,
EDW. ROSE

Both letters are printed, not because they are unique, but because they were usual. From R. C. Carton, John Oliver Hobbes, H. V. Esmond, Stephen Phillips, Haddon Chambers, just such letters came on the eve of and on the day after the first performance.

The Prisoner of Zenda as a play repeated the triumphant success which the novel had won. It was a fine gallant story and Edward Rose had not spoilt it. The play ran for twenty-seven weeks, from January to July 18th, to houses which averaged £200 a performance. And this before the theatre was reconstructed and its seating capacity enlarged. Actually £40,530 : 6 : 7 was the sum taken in at the box-office. The scenery and the dresses were costly. Alexander had spent upon them more than that sum of £3000 which Mr T. Andros de la Rue had been ready to put up for *Hamlet*—£3356 : 7 : 2. And the net profit on the run amounted to £9960 : 10 : 10. In addition Alexander paid himself his salary of about £80 a week. It is difficult to state it more exactly, for in the accounts the salary is set out in

GEORGE ALEXANDER
AS RASSENDYLL IN *THE PRISONER OF ZENDA*

one lump sum for the season—and the season will include perhaps one or two plays with intervals between them, broken weeks, and a varying number of matinees.

But he had not nearly done with *The Prisoner of Zenda*. He took it on tour for eight weeks and reaped from it a net profit of £3486 : 18 : 7. He brought it back to London on October 20th. But by that time its momentary popularity was exhausted. It earned on its fifty-three autumn performances a further profit of £706 : 8 : 11 and was withdrawn on November 28th.

But even then it was not dead and done with. It took its turn in the bill in 1897. It was revived at the St. James' in 1900 and again in 1909. When the accounts of the twenty-six seasons 1890–1916 were made up and audited, the profit earned by *The Prisoner of Zenda* amounted to £18,132 : 2 : 2. This included the profits of tours, from sub-lettings and Alexander's salary whilst acting in the play. It was one of the great successes of the management. *The Importance of Being Earnest*, owing to its triumphant revival in 1910, topped it by nearly £4000, *Bella Donna* by £7000, *The Second Mrs Tanqueray* by £4000. *His House in Order* stood by itself. It was the high-water mark of the management. It ran for fifty-seven weeks in London; two companies carried it through the provinces, Alexander toured it himself. It was revived for seventy-three performances in the autumn of 1914. But the guns were thundering upon Ypres and a people unused to great wars was preparing a vast army and manufacturing its equipment. The trials of an undisciplined wife in a house stiff with rules were not the entertainment for those days. Even so Alexander's total earnings from that comedy rose to the sum of £36,638 : 15 : 4; and this though the author's fees on the London performances were just simply half the profits.

CHAPTER VII

As You Like It · Harry Irving · W. P. Ker's criticisms · Pinero: an appreciation · *The Princess and
the Butterfly* · Pinero and Alexander part company ·
Alexander's domestic life · *The Ambassador* · A first
night in 1900 compared with a first night to-day · Sir
Squire Bancroft · The gallery

ROMANCE succeeded upon romance, and it was in
the fitness of that theatre where so much was fit
that the better should follow upon the good. Shakespeare's comedy *As You Like It* was acted upon
Wednesday, December 2nd, 1896, and with the
exception of one night when Alexander closed the
theatre that he might be present at the Annual
Dinner of the Actors' Benevolent Fund, until March
20th, 1897. One hundred and fourteen performances
were given with average takings of £200 a performance, so that the venture yielded a handsome profit.
Apart from his regular lieutenants, H. H. Vincent,
H. V. Esmond, who was then making up his mind
to devote himself altogether to the writing of plays,
Arthur Royston, Vincent Sternroyd, Henry Loraine,
W. H. Vernon, Alexander strengthened his company
with artists who bore famous names or were soon to
acquire them. James Fernandez played the Banished
Duke, C. Aubrey Smith, who once bowled for
Sussex, afterwards headed the comedy company of
the Haymarket Theatre, and now dignifies every
film from Hollywood which requires an English

III

gentleman, was the Usurper; H. B. Irving acted that ungrateful part of Oliver.

Harry Irving was a many-sided man, and though he rose to a high place amongst the actors of his time, it is doubtful whether he chose his profession wisely. He wrote in his youth an engaging Life of Judge Jeffreys on a plan the very opposite of that which is fashionable to-day. The mode now for the biographer is to strip his subject of those virtues in which time and custom have dressed him, and to show him off as something of a half-wit and a good deal of a rogue. Harry Irving dipped his brush in a pail of good thick whitewash and made of Jeffreys such a judge as we should all like to stand before when we are put upon our trials to answer for our sins; but I doubt but what Dame Alice Lisle would have chosen another and indeed any other at the Bristol Assizes, if she had got the chance. It is perhaps a little strange that Harry Irving should have been moved to so lenient a view of his hero, for he had a sardonic humour and was deeply interested in the study of crime. He was one of the half-dozen enthusiasts who founded The Crimes Club, and would never have missed one of its dinners at the Great Central Hotel, except under the direst compulsion. He was an admirable speaker and he wrote many lucid and penetrating studies of French criminals, whom he found more interesting than the variety which his own country produced. He was a man with a keen classical face which had a touch of Sherlock Holmes in it, and whether from indifference or deliberation I cannot say, in the street he looked the complete tragedian. He was the best of companions, for he had a sharp and at the same time a kindly eye for the oddities of people, and could reduce what he observed to a racy phrase. He could tell, too, a story against himself, the test of a good companion. For instance. He produced the tragedy of *Hamlet*, playing of course the Prince. With a desire to make vivid the scene upon the battlements, in the chill of a winter's night, he set up braziers of coal at which the sentries warmed themselves. He had the deepest veneration for his great father and persuaded him to come and see him at a matinee. He was naturally extremely nervous about Sir Henry's verdict and begged him to come round after the first act. "Well, Father," he asked anxiously, "did you see anything to tell me?" He received the devastating answer, "Yes, my boy. I see that the streets are up in Elsinore."

But this was many years after he played Oliver to Alexander's Orlando. Young Robert Loraine, afterwards a fearless airman and now a leading actor in the United States, was the third of the brothers Jacques de Bois. Bertram Wallis was the Amiens; Julia Neilson the Rosalind. Fay Davis, long associated with the St. James' Theatre, brought her light and sympathetic touch to the part of Celia, and Dorothea Baird, fresh from her triumph as Trilby, was, as Phoebe, nature's no less than Alexander's choice.

The play was seen by W. P. Ker, a great Shakespearian scholar and Professor of English Literature at University College, London, and he joined with the ordinary public in applauding the revival. He wrote in gratitude "for a very well-spent afternoon", with one reservation:

It has been a great pleasure to me to be present at the production of *As You Like It* and I wish to offer my sincere congratulations. I admire the way in which the whole thing hangs together, and especially the way in which the *pastoral* character of the play is brought out. It is what I have been hoping to see for long past.

There is one great fault, as it seems to me, and I hope you will allow me to speak of it. I felt very strongly at the time, and cannot get over the impression, that the Cuckoo Song from "Love's Labour's Lost" has no business in this play, and that coming where it does it spoils one of the most delicate and subtle pieces of drama in the world. It scrawls over all the delicate lines, and puts the emphasis utterly wrong—it was all that Rosalind could do to get the scene back into the proper temper. It seemed to me to undo the whole effect that had been so admirably worked up in the earlier part of the scene. I am afraid that the audience thought differently, but my impression was a very strong one, and I hope that the point may be reconsidered, in the interests of a very beautiful rendering of the most attractive (I think) of Shakespeare's plays.

> Believe me,
> Sincerely yours,
> W. P. KER

For a year or two after this beautiful revival Alexander marked time. A play by Carton, *The Tree of Knowledge*, neither detracted from nor greatly added to its author's reputation. A comedy was extracted from Pinero with much difficulty, but to extract a play from Pinero was always like taking out a very deeply rooted molar except that all the pain was experienced by the dentist. Pinero would oblige any manager by tearing up his contract, but he would not be hurried. He buried himself in his country house at North Chapel on the border between Sussex and Surrey and until the work was finished— not to his satisfaction, for I think that never happened, but as nearly to his satisfaction as he could hope to get—he would not budge. It would be to the manager's advantage as surely as to his own that he should take his time. In a letter concerning his most successful play *His House in Order*, at a time when there was a strong and special reason to drive him along, he wrote:

I can't *hurry*; that paralyses me. I have taken enormous pains over the thing, as I know you will believe; and when it is complete it will appear—I hope—as if it were a week's work. Which is what I understand by technique.

In some instances, however, his labours produced an effect the very opposite. In the construction of his plays, I suppose that he was as great a master as the English stage has possessed.

I wish I could have sent you Act 3—which is progressing famously—at the same time, so that you could have seen at the first glance how every hint and every clue contained in the earlier acts are followed up and rounded off.

He had a theme, a story, characters to tell it, and a plan, a sort of geometrical figure within the confining lines of which all had to be made natural and clear, so natural that a spectator should not be dissatisfied, so clear that he should not be puzzled. The sequence of scenes must seem inevitable; the people in an age which knows not "front-cloths", must somehow come into the action of the play and be

found upon the stage without calling the attention
of the audience to the mechanism of their entrances
and exits; and each word they speak must not only
help to reveal their individualities, but must have an
intention which will only be completely recognised
when the story is at its end. I have never known a
dramatist who did not ungrudgingly acknowledge
that of this difficult art of construction Pinero was
the supreme master in his generation. Foolish people
catching at a phrase have used that mastery to
diminish him. He was the craftsman, they say, and
nothing more. Was there ever depreciation so wit-
less? The man who could take a Dean who, not
having a penny, offers a thousand pounds towards
the restoration of his cathedral on condition that
nine others do the same, and then finds to his dismay
that there are nine others, and build out of his
predicament so gorgeous a farce as *Dandy Dick*, is
not to be relegated to the back benches of craftsmen.
Is it not the power to pluck the meaning out of the
ordinary things of life and while keeping them true
giving them universality and permanence which is
the sign manual of the artist? The author of *The
Second Mrs Tanqueray*, of *His House in Order*, of a
greatly underrated play *The Enchanted Cottage*, to
name only three, takes his place by right in that high
class. I don't know how many have read an unacted
tragedy by Pinero called *Dr. Harmer's Holidays*, the
story of a grim case of the *nostalgie de la boue*, but
those who have will put down the cheap criticism
that he was merely a first-class mechanic at its proper
value.

His fault was that he laboured overmuch upon the

words which he put into his characters' mouths.
Whether it was that he was minded to give them a
literary varnish, who shall say? The most likely
explanation is that he went back and rewrote and
went back again and rewrote, until his judgment was
lost and drowned in the ocean of his vocabulary.
What was simple began to look flat and to need
ornament. His methods of work suggest that the
reason is to be found in them. He took the air in
the morning and withdrew to his study in the afternoon, and thence the hours until bedtime were given
more often than not without a break to his play.
The habit of overloading his sentences grew upon
him. In the earlier farces and plays the dialogue was
as direct as dialogue could be. When there was
exaggeration it was the comic exaggeration proper
to the kind of play. But in the later plays, *Letty* for
instance especially, this one blemish of making his
characters speak ornate periphrases which no mortal
man would use, and no actor could deliver without
becoming artificial, did a lot to obscure his great
qualities as a dramatist.

The Princess and the Butterfly, which followed
As You Like It on March 29th of the year 1897, dealt,
in its author's words, "with the struggle of middle
age with love". It dealt a little over-importantly
with a not very important theme. Alexander played
one of those parts of men in the forties which he was
beginning to make his own. Sir George Lamorant
was easy work compared with Aubrey Tanqueray.
The part required dignity, tenderness, humour,
anger, but it made nothing like a strong call upon
his emotional power. It was, moreover, rather sen-

tentious, and his consciousness of his age was so dwelt upon in his speeches that it needed all the actor's skill to avoid an impression of trifling egotism. Julia Neilson played an Hungarian Princess who was equally but with more semblance of reason distressed by the flight of her youth, and Fay Davis, in the character of a wayward half-Italian untutored waif, had an opportunity of which she made full use.

The play makes strange reading to-day. Middle-age is an obsession. The introduction of a woman with a past into a group amongst whom is Sir George's ward is matter for a duel. The woman with a past has poured the burgundy into her finger-bowl. Actually she has done that! The girl, Fay Zuliani, slips out of the house, having no latchkey, with another girl and goes off dressed as a Harlequin to the masked ball at the Opera House. It is an escapade so disreputable that it must be hidden even from the servants. We are presented with a picture of the times as remote from these days as those middle ages which were not the theme of the play. One cannot but ask oneself, "Are these the naughty nineties?" But even at that date it was considered that the author's picture of the times was over-coloured and the moral overstressed. There were to be sure effective scenes and some diverting satire upon the youth of the day; and what with Pinero's reputation and the high position which Alexander had won both by his acting and his management of his theatre, and the proficiency of his company, the play ran for nearly a hundred nights. Although the cast was very large and strewn with the big names of the day,

H. B. Irving, H. V. ⸻d, A. Vane Tempest,
Julia Neilson, Pattie ⸻lie Opp, Fay Davis,
Rose Leclercq, a hundre⸻rmances were enough
as a rule to ensure a r⸻le profit at the St.
James'. But the play wa⸻e acts and needed
elaborate scenery, whilst ⸻ of the characters
with only a line or so to s⸻d to speak them
in costly uniforms. The exp⸻ the production,
which exceeded that of *As Y⸻ It* by a couple
of hundred pounds, swallow⸻ as much again
as the profit on the actual playir⸻ended in a loss
of nearly two thousand pounds.

The rehearsals of this play did⸻n smoothly.
The crowded stage during the sec⸻d third acts
must have taxed even so resource⸻roducer as
Alexander. Differences of opinion⸻n Pinero
and Alexander became acute, not fo⸻rst time,
but the personal friendship between⸻vo men
was not spoilt.

Part of the literary jargon of that ⸻s the
phrase, "a human document". It was t⸻ out
to extinction by over-use. But it describes⸻fitly
the correspondence which follows here. It seems to
me that anyone who keeps in mind that after all this
smashing-up for ever and ever of old associations,
actor and author were to combine in making the
greatest success of their lives, cannot but read it with
amusement or indeed with a warm friendliness for
both of them. Pinero was so determined, Alexander
so remorseful. Never again were they to work together on the stage of the St. James'. No, never!
And nine years actually did elapse before *His House
in Order* was produced.

The first letter was written by Alexander on December 21st, 1896, from Ovingdean:

MY DEAR P.,

I hope you got my brief wire of delight on reading the play. It is wonderful—simply wonderful, and exceeds my highest hopes; interesting—absorbingly interesting, especially in the last three acts. That fourth act—for direct humanity, perfection of workmanship, and sheer brilliancy of intellectuality and power equals anything you have ever done.

The last act, too, is startling in its genius, with its manipulation of "the fairy tale happy for ever after" ending —it fairly takes one's breath away: it is so delicate, so profound and so limitlessly human in its analysis.

Do you care to come here with me for a Sunday in January? If so I should be delighted—any Sunday except the 17th.

I've seen Telbin and arranged with him for the last scene; he will have the model done early in Jany., when I'll get you to look at it.

Every good wish to Mrs Pin and yourself: we are here till Friday.

Yours,
ALEC

To this Pinero replied:

MY DEAR ALEC,

I was pleased to receive your telegram (which I ought to have acknowledged) and am more than pleased to read this morning, in your kind letter, the very warm expressions you employ in reference to *The Princess and the Butterfly*. There are no pleasanter moments for the playwright than those in which he finds his manager in full sympathy and accord with him.

Could gratitude be warmer, or the reply to it more cordial? With day-to-day rehearsals letters are not to be expected, but one which Pinero wrote during the course of them suggests the turn which things were taking.

I am sure you are quite wise to take it easy to-morrow. And, anyhow, you need have no concern for your strictly personal share in the forthcoming new show; your rehearsals convince me that Sir George Lamorant will be a very striking figure and a most charming fellow into the bargain.

The play, however, was not enthusiastically received, and though it played to houses averaging £160 a night, it only did so because Alexander took it off when the receipts began to drop. Alexander, when the rehearsals were over, seems to have been unaware that they had left a sting in Pinero's sensibilities which ached even three years afterwards. For he wrote to Pinero from Cromer in the autumn of 1899 without a suspicion that any misunderstanding existed:

MY DEAR PINERO,

Would you care to have the autumn opening date for a play at the new St. James' next year? If so I would give up my tour, and begin work at whatever time you thought best. I think you will like the new theatre—it will hold about £35 a performance more, and still, I hope, be small enough for any play. The de la Rues write me that you are expected at Maloja. I have had a delightful holiday and am quite well again. I return to London on the 15th and could see you if you thought anything of this proposal.

Yours sincerely,
GEORGE ALEXANDER

This innocent letter called forth some pleasant friendly phrases first and the thunderbolt afterwards:

MY DEAR ALEC,

I am glad to hear from you and to know that you have had an enjoyable and restful holiday. For myself, business has kept me in town much later than I care for; but we are off on Saturday morning to our old haunt—Maloja. Somewhere about Sept. 12th we shall drop down to Cadenabbia; thence I go to Turin, (to assist at the production, in Italian, of Quex! an odd experience) and finally, to amuse my stepdaughter, to Venice. All being well I shall be home again by the middle of October.

Accept my hearty thanks, dear Alec, for your suggestion that I should write a play for the opening of your remodelled theatre. I have such pleasurable associations with the old house that I cannot reconcile myself to the title—the *New* St. James's. May it, at any rate, resemble the old in the fame and fortune it brings its tenant.

Coming to the dry bones of your proposal, I consider it best to be quite open and candid with you. If my words bear a curt and abrupt look pray ascribe it to the limitations imposed by a hurriedly-written letter. Frankly, dear Alec, I don't think that you and I go well together in harness; or, rather, I do not feel happy in running tandem with you, myself as wheeler to your lead. I know you take a pride in being an autocrat in your theatre; it is a natural pride in a position which you have worthily won for yourself. But I also have won—or have chosen to usurp—a similarly autocratic position in all that relates to my work. I hope I do not use my power unfairly or overbearingly, but I do exercise it—and any other condition of things is intolerable to me. In my association with you on the stage I have always felt that you have resented my authority. In the case of our last joint venture the circumstances which led up to it were

of so unhappy a character that I resolved to abrogate this
authority—to reduce it, at any rate, to a shadow. But, at the
same time, I did not relish my position and determined—
even before I started upon a campaign which I foresaw could
not be otherwise than full of discomfort and constraint—
that I would not again occupy it. To put the case shortly,
there is not room for two autocrats in one small kingdom;
and in every detail, however slight, that pertains to my
work—though I avail myself gratefully of any assistance
that is afforded me—I take to myself the right of dictation
and veto.

In face of this explanation, my dear Alec, (longer than I
intended it to be) I trust you will forgive me for declining
your offer, and will believe that this prompt candour on my
part is exhibited in a spirit of fairness to yourself as well as
from a desire to explain my own attitude.

Notwithstanding the foregoing, I am, I assure you, none
the less obliged to you for your proposal. By making it you
pay me a compliment, one I appreciate thoroughly.

I am, my dear Alec,

Yours always truly,

ARTHUR W. PINERO

Thus with every expression of friendship and good-
will—and no one who knew anything of Pinero's
reticence and his warmth of heart could doubt the
sincerity of that expression—Pinero in 1897 had
finished with the St. James' Theatre. The memory
of the rehearsals of *The Princess and the Butterfly*
still rankled after two years. The two men who together had done so much to lift the theatre to a
higher place in the estimation of intelligent people,
were henceforth to go different ways. It was a great
pity. Or rather, it would have been a great pity for

them and for the public had the decision stood. It is possible that Alexander did not take it so tragically. He was well acquainted by now with the irritable race of authors. Had he not remained on happy terms with the most violent of them all, Henry Arthur Jones? He had the patience of his Scotch blood, and could wait even thrice two years. He wrote in reply to Pinero on August 11th:

MY DEAR P.,

Thank you for your very kind letter. I appreciate all you say, and you worthily deserve the position you "usurp". My new theatre reopens in Jany. and it was of the autumn 1900 that I wrote. I now quite understand what you demand in regard to your work and should be willing to welcome you at the St. James' under that understanding. I daresay I did not realise this before, and indeed you did not ask it of me. Please pardon me for this. I am sure we could work together should you feel willing to give it a trial. Don't bother to answer this, but sometime I hope to have a line from you saying "Yes".

Give my love to the de la Rues: I have not spoken to them about this matter.

Our united regards to Mrs Pinero and yourself. Even if we never work together again believe me I value your regard and am   Always yours sincerely,

GEORGE ALEXANDER

In the autumn he replaced *The Princess and the Butterfly* with R. C. Carton's play *The Tree of Knowledge*, which ran successfully for sixteen weeks.

These were pleasant years for the Alexanders. They had a host of friends, old and new; amongst the new the Duke of Fife, Lord and Lady St. Helier,

Wylie Mathews the Government Prosecutor, Field-Marshal Sir Evelyn Wood, Sir Hubert Herkomer, Sir George Lewis, and an ample social life of which Mrs Alexander bore the weight. They had an unclouded home and a theatre which had become known outside England for good plays, good acting, and scrupulous attention to detail. Henry Irving in a speech at a supper party in the Beefsteak Room at the Lyceum had lectured the young couple for rushing into management before they had learned to do more than totter; and afterwards with the kindness he had for them, he promised to keep Alexander's place in the Lyceum Company open for him for eight months. They had been established now at the St. James' for eight years. Alexander was still under forty, and with all deference to Sir George Lamorant, rather approaching the full opportunities of his life, and the fullness of his power to use them, than on the threshold of his decline; and he had the pleasure of exercising a wide and private generosity. At one time an author ill and down on his luck, who never had done and never was to do any work for the St. James' Theatre, obtains his first glimpse of the Rhine; an old friend finds the world the easier for having the annual premiums of his life assurance guaranteed; a journalist is helped by letter and spoken word to a high position on an important newspaper. Authors who were hard pressed found their advance fees repeated. Loans which were never to be returned were made and written off. Alexander was on the councils of the Actors' Benevolent and Royal General Theatrical Funds. His own art and the Associations which supported it were always foremost in his thoughts and plans. He was later on to be a Vice-President of the Actors' Association. When he became a knight he received a telegram of congratulation from Israel Zangwill. But that sea-green Incorruptible was careful to state that the telegram did not come from any recognition of Alexander's merit, either as actor or producer, but was due entirely to the fact that he was President of the Actresses' Franchise League. His craft stood first with him, and when at the beginning of the war a brilliant publicist and editor compared the Kaiser to an actor-manager, Alexander protested with so firm and quiet a dignity that the publicist, on the verge of pleading that there was a flamboyancy common to both which justified his parallel, found it more reasonable to admit that his words were unfair.

These middle years were busy ones and pleasant ones. He had his troubles, of course, like other men. He was very sensitive and easily hurt; and when he was hurt, something had got to be done about it. If Pinero, who hated parties, slipped away from one without greeting Alexander, he had to explain at length that it was not any coldness in his affection which had made him bolt. If H. V. Esmond left the theatre on the last night of his successful play *The Wilderness*, without saying good-bye to Alexander because Alexander was the centre of a crowd, that too had got to be made clear. If Sutro read to a friend a play which Alexander was going to produce, without letting Alexander know, this was—not a breach of etiquette, but a neglect of friendship. If at times Alexander showed a certain aloofness, as he

GEORGE ALEXANDER
AS BENEDICK IN *MUCH ADO ABOUT NOTHING*

undoubtedly did, it was the aloofness of a man who was easily hurt, and cultivated a manner of reticence in consequence.

In the theatre he had his failures. But they came inevitably to make up the complete chequer-board of life: *The Conquerors*, a bad affair by Paul M. Potter, dramatic carpenter-in-chief to Charles Frohman, who fudged it up out of a couple of short masterpieces by Guy de Maupassant; *Rupert of Hentzau*, which with its conclusion in death and requiem accorded too poignantly with the first months of the Boer War. Do people remember now, with the experiences of 1914–1918 behind them, how a casualty list of a thousand killed and wounded at the end of a battle, made people gasp with horror and amazement? Or how the orderly grief-stricken throng gathered at night about the notice-boards outside the War Office in Pall Mall? The Royal Automobile Club stands now where those notice-boards with their lists of killed and wounded were hung. And *Rupert of Hentzau* was amongst the casualties. On the other hand John Oliver Hobbes, as Mrs Pearl Mary-Teresa Craigie preferred to be known, wrote for the St. James' a delicate, effective and successful comedy in *The Ambassador*; H. V. Esmond, who never quite realised all of his great promise, hit the mark with *The Wilderness*; Walter Frith, son of the famous artist, added *A Man of Forty*. Alexander put on perhaps the best of all Shakespeare's comedies, *Much Ado About Nothing*. I say "perhaps" in deference to W. P. Ker's preference for *As You Like It*, already quoted. *Much Ado* was not as well suited either to Alexander himself or to the company, as had been *As You Like It*, and fifty-three performances exhausted its popularity. But the management was never at a loss now for a bill to replace a failure. The times were not yet ripe for revivals of *Lady Windermere's Fan* or *The Importance of Being Earnest*. But *Liberty Hall*, *The Idler*, *The Second Mrs Tanqueray*, *The Prisoner of Zenda*, were always ready at the shortest notice. And even those plays which did not gain the suffrages of the London playgoers had the verdict reversed on an appeal to the provinces. *Rupert of Hentzau*, who gained nothing and cost nothing upon the London venture, made nearly £3000 on the tours. And *The Princess and the Butterfly*, which resulted in London in a net loss of seventeen hundred and ninety-eight pounds-odd, ended with a profit of seven hundred and ninety-four. To use a simile more than usually appropriate, what Alexander lost on the swings, he made on the roundabouts. His theatre was seldom shut on these autumn tours. He had a devoted staff to leave behind, so that those who hired the St. James' from him during his absences could be certain that their plans would be carried out with the same smoothness and the same meticulous care as the lessee insisted upon for himself. Thus at the conclusion of the run of *The Elder Miss Blossom*, which the Kendals produced at the St. James' Theatre on September 16th, 1901, W. H. Kendal was able to write:

My dear Alexander,

I take the first opportunity—now you are back—of writing to *thank* you for having made us so comfortable during our too brief season at your Theatre, and to say what a very pleasant time we had there—enhanced, not a little, by the uniform courtesy and attention of all the Staff both before and behind the curtain—and I took on all your old hands. I never had occasion to utter a single word of complaint in any one department—on the contrary, only words of commendation! And it gives me great pleasure to record this fact.

I am glad that everything was found satisfactory on our quitting the theatre and nothing to mar an altogether most gratifying little season—in more ways than one. And which has added another to the many pleasant memories we must always associate with the St. James' Theatre.

§

After the failure of Mr Potter's medley *The Conquerors*, a comedy by John Oliver Hobbes was put on, called *The Ambassador*. The date was June 2nd, 1898. It was a late hour of the London season for a new play. Moreover the theatre had been let to the Kendals for the autumn and Alexander had arranged a long tour for himself with a heavy repertoire. There remained, then, no more than seven weeks before the St. James' would be closed. But during those seven weeks from June 2nd to July 22nd, the comedy so caught the taste of the town that it was played to an average taking of £217 a performance. It was the very play for the St. James' Theatre. Its name alone, with George Alexander in the title-rôle, was almost a sufficient lure. A play of pink candle-shades and beautiful dresses and George Alexander as British Ambassador at Rome with the red ribbon of the Bath across his white waistcoat; the odds were four to one on that *The Ambassador* would be a winner in the steeplechase of a theatrical venture. Outer London would flock to it in any case. Inner London, too, if the authoress sustained in the theatre the reputation she had made for herself with her novels. And she did.

Mrs Pearl Mary-Teresa Craigie lived with her father, a wealthy American, in Lancaster Gate. She lived in a tall house and wrote short books. They were clever rather than profound, but she wrote very well in an epigrammatic and allusive style, with an economy of adjectives and dialogue in which the meaning was at once condensed and clear. She was in addition an intimate friend of the Alexanders and an enthusiastic admirer of his acting. She had, too, the advantage of one of those excellent casts which had come to be expected at this theatre: H. B. Irving, H. V. Esmond, Fred Terry amongst the men, Violet Vanbrugh, Fay Davis, Mary Jerrold, Kate Sargeantson, amongst the women. The story of the play was slight but strong enough. The characters represented by Alexander and Fay Davis bore a noticeable likeness to those which they had represented in *The Princess and the Butterfly*, but they were less superficial. The language which they spoke was more natural and direct and Fay Davis was not handicapped by a broken accent. Mrs Craigie, according to Sir Sidney Lee in the *Dictionary of National Biography*, was guilty of some incoherence in the plot and character-isation. The plot stood upon its feet well enough, but the party at the beginning of the third act in Major Lascelles' rooms was a bewildering affair and Major Lascelles himself was a tangle of ragged ends. The dialogue, however, except in the case of this one scene, was witty without the appearance of effort. You were never left with the impression that the authoress had got her characters together at this or that given moment and adjured herself "Now they have just got to be witty. So what shall I make them say?" Scenes between men alone have no doubt been the salvation of many plays; and they have been written by men. Mrs Craigie, being a woman and an observant woman, took a leaf out of their books and rewrote it in a novel fashion. She introduced some scenes between women alone, and the amusement which they afforded did much at the beginning of the play to set the audience in a favourable mood. Alexander had a part to his liking. He was partly the *raisonneur* of the French comedies, and partly the man of the world stirred unexpectedly to a depth of emotion and romance of which he had not believed himself capable. Mrs Craigie dedicated the published book of the play to him, and ended her preface to it with a graceful tribute to his skill:

My permanent gratitude and friendship are due to Mr. George Alexander for the distinguished art he bestowed upon his rendering of the title-rôle, for the support, interest, and kindness he gave so generously from the first reading of the play, through the many anxieties of rehearsing, to the yet greater anxiety of its first production.

A charming scene with a surprise in the best vein of comedy brought the curtain down to laughter and unreserved applause. The critics were not impressed though it was impossible to say that this was not a St. James' play, and the verdict of the public was repeated one hundred and sixty-three times in

London and endorsed by the substantial signature of the Provinces.

The Ambassador was the last successful play produced by George Alexander at the old theatre. He had hoped, with his experience of *The Prisoner of Zenda* to encourage him, to put up Edward Rose's adaptation of Stanley Weyman's novel *Under the Red Robe*. But Rose argued that it offered too insufficient an opportunity for the leading actor and persuaded him instead to produce a costly piece of fustian, called *In Days of Old*, which was withdrawn after sixty-one performances. Alexander, then, that is in the summer of the year 1899, set out upon a provincial tour of eighteen weeks, whilst the theatre was handed over to the decorators and builders.

On February 1st, 1900, the St. James' Theatre was reopened. Except for the colder scheme of colour upon the walls and the conversion of Alexander's long room and the dressing-room which opened out of it, into offices, it is now much what it was upon that night. The play was *Rupert of Hentzau*, Anthony Hope's own version of his sequel to *The Prisoner of Zenda*.

A first night at a theatre in the year 1900 was an event in the social life of the town. There are too many of them in 1935 to arouse more than a languid interest, unless something special in the way of a big drum is beaten cunningly for a long time ahead. Also there are too few men and women acting in their own theatres. The theatre is now accommodation for a play. In 1900 it was that and a good deal more. It was definitely associated with someone, an old friend as it were, who for good or ill had chosen

the play which the audience was now to see, who
would himself or herself shortly appear upon the
boards. It was more vital on that account. It was less
of a lodging-house. There was a thrill in the air as
the auditorium filled. Would the old firm do it again?
Was this new playwright going to make his mark?
There was expectation, even a trifle of excitement
before the lights went out and the overture began.
The horseshoe shape of the auditorium contributed
to produce that rapport between the actors behind
the footlights and the spectators in front of them
which is essential to the enjoyment of a play. There
were people everywhere—people and warm colours.
A spark passed from one to another and established
a sort of fellowship which would last the evening
through. Inconveniences no doubt existed. Certain
seats at the tips of the horn of the dress-circle could
not be or ought not to have been used. But the more
recent theatres with their blank side walls and chilly
colours beget a certain aloofness in the audience.
It is more detached.

In the stalls of the St. James' a distinguished company would gather. Lord and Lady St. Helier (then
Sir Francis and Lady Jeune), Sir Hubert Herkomer,
Sir Anderson Critchett the oculist, the Duke and
Duchess of Fife, all looking to find their pleasure
in the success of the play. There would be others
who hoped to find their pleasure in the failure of the
play. Captain Robert Marshall, the author of *His
Excellency the Governor*, entering the supper-room
of his club late one night amidst a burst of laughter
said, "I see from the general hilarity that you have
all been assisting at the first night of some appalling

fiasco". Such eager ill-wishers are still to be found in
the stalls of any theatre on a first night. Their race,
like the worm, dieth not. And aloof amongst them
all, well-wishers and ill-wishers, sat the formidable
phalanx of the critics. Each one solemn as the Doge
of Venice and pledged, it seemed, that neither smile
nor tear nor any expression of content or discontent
should anticipate the judgment which his newspaper
would reveal in the morning. And often would be
noticed against the glow of the lighted scene the
picturesque head and fine white hair of Sir Squire
Bancroft as he crossed the theatre to his seat in the
front row of the stalls just a fraction of time after
the curtain had gone up on the opening of the third
act. Sir Squire Bancroft was in his place at the St.
James' Theatre. For as Irving developed the example
of a suitable decoration for the classic plays which
had been set by Edmund Kean, so Alexander in his
settings of his modern comedies followed and per-
fected the model and pattern of the Bancrofts. Sir
Squire was not content, as his predecessors had been,
merely to call a room a room, he built it on the stage;
and though he retired from the management of the
Haymarket Theatre at an age when most managers
are beginning, he had already made a revolution in
the theatre. No one did more to kill bombast and
the heroics of Alonzo and Gonzago than the manager
who gave an opportunity to Tom Robertson.
Though he had long since ceased to act or manage
in 1900, Bancroft was a known and noticeable personage. With his black-rimmed eyeglass on a black
ribbon of watered silk, his mass of white hair and
his broad flat-brimmed silk hat, he had something

of the dandy in him. He lived at A.1 Albany—where else could he have lived?—and when not bespoken, he lunched at the Garrick Club and dined at the Athenaeum. Every morning, tall and upright to the end of his long life, he would walk from Albany to his bank in St. James' Street, hand a slip of paper across the counter to a clerk and ask, "Is that my balance this morning?" Assured that his figures were correct, he went upon his way. Stories so clustered about him that at times you could hardly see the man for them. But most of them were based upon some shrewd comment which he might have made. He and Pinero were great cronies, well aware of each other's foibles and not slow to describe them; and rightly or wrongly, a good many of those not un-kindly stories were attributed to the invention of Pinero. Of two, however, I know. Sir Squire Ban-croft was a Victorian to the marrow of his bones. He had the Victorian passion for funerals; a wreath for his acquaintances, a wreath and his presence at the graveside for his friends. I met him one day wearing the habiliments of woe. He said to me with the due mournfulness: "I have just been to Golders Green. I had never attended a cremation before. The relatives were kind enough afterwards to ask me to go behind." At another time—it was the day following the first performance of *The Admirable Crichton*, the fine comedy by Barrie in which the sentiment is so brilliantly mitigated by a healthful sharp touch of acid. I asked, having seen him at the performance, what he thought of the play. He was drying his hands on his towel in the lavatory of his club just before luncheon. He dried more slowly and shook his head with melancholy. "It deals, my dear Mason, with the juxtaposition of the drawing-room and the servants' hall—always to me a very painful subject."

It seemed to me that I heard the whole of that era, the Manchester school, as well as the squires of the counties, the merchants of the City of London as well as the dames of Kensington and Mayfair, all epitomised and defined in that one unexpected sentence.

Apart from Sir Squire and the visitors to the stalls and the dress-circle and the patrons of the drama in the upper circle and the pit, there was another element in the fortunes of a play which, if no more powerful, was louder in giving an adverse verdict than it is to-day—the gallery. The gallery generally waited, as it rightfully should, to the end of the play, before it announced its high decision; and sometimes it was guilefully able to lure an unhappy author on to the stage unaware of the greeting which awaited him. I passed about this time the exit from the gallery of a theatre where Henry Arthur Jones had that night had a play produced which had failed. I heard one youth exclaim to his friends indignantly, "Why didn't the fellow come out and take his punishment?" and I marvelled at the odd point of view. The youth had spent a shilling and I felt sure had enjoyed himself prodigiously. Henry Arthur Jones, on the other hand, had spent the best part of a year toiling over his play, and had seen all his work fritter away to nothing within the compass of three hours. Why, in addition, should he trot forward on the stage and bow to a storm of booing and hissing?

There was an epidemic of it at the time. It is quite true, of course, that an audience at a play has no concern in the troubles of authorship, the strain of rehearsals, the costliness of the setting, the difficulties of the company. There is no compulsion upon the author to write, the producer to rehearse, the manager to stage the play, or the actors to act it. The audience is concerned with the result. But also there is no compulsion upon the playgoer to attend the first performance. He can wait, if he likes, until he learns from the newspapers or his acquaintances whether he is likely to get enjoyment in return for his shilling or whether he is not. The theory of a vociferous punishment is untenable on any grounds of reason and justice; and the theatre to-day is the better for the disuse of it.

CHAPTER VIII

THE reconstruction of the theatre during the autumn of 1899 cost £7057 : 14 : 6, a large hole in the savings of a theatrical management however prudent the administration had been. But Alexander had the courage to spend money, just as he had had the courage to put on in a theatre which drew its patrons from the ordered society of the day a play which challenged its very code and made a moving tragedy out of the inflexibility of its conditions. He had hoped to reopen the St. James' with a new play by Pinero, but Pinero, though still and always a great personal friend of Alexander's, was in the mood to have nothing to do—no, not if he lived to the age of Methuselah—with the autocratic manager. "My dear Alec" and he couldn't avoid a stately dog-fight when between them they produced a play. Alexander fell back upon *Rupert of Hentzau*, Anthony Hope's own adaptation of his novel. Sequels, however, are ticklish things. The spirit has too often evaporated, the first fine flavour of enthusiasm as the story and its characters swam into view, altogether gone and

138

beyond recapture. As it was with the book, so it was with the play. Old Sapt and Fritz von Tarlenheim had aged, Rudolf himself had grown sedate. The play ended with a requiem and Rudolf lying in state. It matched too well with the sadness of the times. It ran for eight weeks, and for the second time in the history of the management a play cost nothing and earned nothing. After the first three weeks, matinees of *The Prisoner of Zenda* eked it out and brought into the treasury a small profit.

Alexander substituted for it on March 28th a play by Walter Frith called *The Man of Forty* and it ran with moderate success until July 6th. Young Dennis Eadie, who was afterwards to become the manager of the Royalty Theatre in Dean Street, restore it to prosperity, and produce a notable play by Arnold Bennett and Edward Knoblock, *Milestones*, made on this occasion his first appearance at the St. James'.

That year of 1900 Alexander did not go out on tour. He closed his theatre early in July, took a holiday, and reopened in September. He held his lease directly from the proprietors of the theatre and paid a rent which allowed him the rest and change of scene which keep the body and mind of man at working pitch. Is there a theatre held to-day upon those terms? Profit rentals make such tenancies the legends of a golden age. If the actual proprietor receives £100 a week, the man or woman who puts on and acts the play will pay £250, or as much more as can be extracted out of his ignorance or his self-confidence; and that extra sum means that he can never lease a theatre for a term of years, give to it a character of its own, make his long plans ahead, and from time to time under the urgency of nature rest for a while from his labours. The drones won't have that. "Work's for the workman", as Haddon Chambers made his tramp explain in *Passers-By* when he refused a job. On September 1st Alexander produced a play by Sydney Grundy called *A Debt of Honour*. And at once a storm broke out in the theatrical Press. It was the old question of plagiarism. Mrs W. K. Clifford, a well-known authoress, had written a play called *The Likeness of the Night*, which had been accepted by the Kendals and was intended to form the chief feature of their autumn tour. Mr and Mrs Kendal were present at the first performance of *A Debt of Honour* and were astonished by the resemblance between the two plays. Their long experience of the stage, however, enabled them to take note of that resemblance with a philosophic calm. They brought no hurried accusation of plagiarism against Grundy, and were concerned, whilst expressing a hope to Alexander that the to-do might be of help to his play, with the question whether they should or should not postpone their production of *The Likeness of the Night*. Kendal quoted Lord Dundreary, "It's one of those things no fellah can understand", and left it at that. Mrs Clifford, gravely troubled though she was—for as she justly wrote, she made her living by her pen—was careful to absolve Alexander from any suggestion of double dealing. She had negotiated with him before on the subject of another play, and had seen enough of him to be certain of his honesty. It remained for Clement Scott to dip his pen in a potful of malice and insinuate—he dared go no further—a charge against the management. He revived the dispute concerning *The Second Mrs Tanqueray* for his share in which he had already eaten the humblest pie baked in the office of George Lewis, and misstated it—to misstate is the politer word of the two. Now came this second case. Why did these things happen always at the St. James' Theatre? Was there a ghost there who whispered the plots of other authors' plays to playwrights hard up for an idea? And so on.

The insinuation was just as venomous as that picturesque journalist could make it; and it was probably also libellous. But Clement Scott was clever as well as picturesque; and there were saving sentences dropped into the invective which he would have pleaded to show that he was a mere seeker after truth. In any case Clement Scott was not worth a blank cartridge. One hears that there was a time when a column of his writing made or damned a play; so keen was his interest in the theatre, so romantically he wrote about it. But he had grown cantankerous, he showed too publicly his private antipathies, he was no longer the reliable guide, and perhaps A. B. Walkley was educating readers to look for a little more scholarship and a more delicate choice of words than were to be found in the flamboyant sonorities of Clement Scott. An action for libel could have served no purpose; except perhaps to prove with what unusual care the manuscripts of plays were handled in the St. James' Theatre. When a play was received, the date of its arrival and its title were entered in a book. In its turn the play was read. If it was a play for which Alexander had asked, or one which for this or that reason aroused expectation, he read it himself. If he liked it and thought it suitable, he accepted it. If he was in doubt, he submitted it, before definitely making up his mind, to the judgment of someone else whose opinion he esteemed. Thus the play *John Ferguson*, by St. John Ervine, which later on was to make its mark at the little Hammersmith Theatre under the management of Nigel Playfair, was submitted to E. F. Spence, the King's Counsel and at one time the dramatic critic of the *Westminster Gazette*. Both Alexander and Spence assessed it at its true high value, but both doubted the fitness of the times. It arrived in the thick of the war; and tragic realities were too common in daily life to be easily tolerable on the stage. *The Bing Boys* held the field. St. John Ervine has told me that he was deeply distressed to get his play back with the intimation that it could not be done. It was his first real bid for the wider public, and if you will show me a dramatist who is content with anything less, I will show you one who is less than second-rate. But he received a long and sympathetic letter from Alexander the next day which restored his spirits. There can be little doubt that both the King's Counsel and the manager were right, and reserved for the play a happier fate than it would have met with in that year of gloom.

But the play was returned. And when a play was returned, the date of its return was entered in the book, with a few particulars as to its theme. The system was invaluable to authors whose plays were produced at the St. James'. Nothing is more common than a charge of plagiarism. Nothing is more difficult

to disprove. The angry rejected read a favourable
review. They sit down and dash off a letter. The
manager has taken their beautiful plays and handed
them over to this or that miserable scribbler who
has got a name, God knows how, and he has mangled
them until they can hardly be recognised. The book
was then turned up and it was generally found that
the beautiful play had been returned to its owner
months or years even before the miserable scribbler
had appeared upon the doorstep.

The case of Mrs Clifford, however, was on a
different plane. She was a lady of high distinction
and the centre of a cultured circle. Casual accusa-
tions were not amongst the possibilities. But—and
here was the trouble—*The Likeness of the Night* had
been published, a year before, in the *Anglo-Saxon
Review*, an elaborate magazine published quarterly
under the editorship of Lady Randolph Churchill.
The Kendals had made a contract with Mrs Clifford
for the rights of the play, after reading it in the
Review. Mrs Clifford could have brought, no doubt,
an action against Sydney Grundy, who was after all
better known as an adapter than as an original playwright. But just as plagiarism is difficult to disprove,
so it is almost impossible to prove. A very little ingenuity and a good deal of hard swearing and the
plagiarist is safe. Happily both plays were successful.
Sydney Grundy's ran until half way through
November. Eighty-three performances could yield
some small profit to the theatre and more than £500
to the playwright. *The Likeness of the Night* was produced at the same theatre on October 28th of the
following year, 1901, and gave to Mrs Kendal scenes

of pathos and tenderness of which she made superb use.

Alexander brought one of his least successful years, the year 1900, to its finish with a comedy by Mrs Craigie (John Oliver Hobbes) named *The Wisdom of the Wise*. It was produced on November 22nd, and when the curtain fell the gallery made so obstreperous a demonstration that even the Press raised protests against this overweening assumption of authority. A question of concerted action on the part of the managers was raised. The proposal that critics should be invited to the dress-rehearsal was debated, and I believe that for a time one or two managers closed their galleries upon first nights. But exhibitions of so violent a kind have ceased even to be the exception nowadays. I expect that those who made up that small but vociferous portion of the audience prefer the dog-tracks nowadays. They can at all events get a dog-fight from time to time without having to take part in it themselves.

The Wisdom of the Wise lasted out no more than fifty-four performances and was withdrawn on January 12th of 1901. The play was designed on a well-tried notion of comedy—the effort of a group of discontented people to make mischief between two couples who, left to themselves, were entirely happy. The fault of the play was that the mischief-makers made no mischief. They were too incompetent, and the few misunderstandings which were their raw material were too flimsy to bear the weight of their endeavours and too theatrically conventional to create any illusion of reality in the audience. The one necessity in a play, the necessity of suspense, was completely absent and the action was not helped by the introduction of one of those fatuous snobs who used to figure as members of parliament in the social comedies of the day. Mr Bradgers-De-Lisle-Bradgers came not out of Mrs Craigie's keen observation of men and women. He was a stuffed figure and the sawdust was running out of him long before she made him pay a midnight call at a house where he was unknown, to interview a duke whom he didn't know.

Mrs Craigie took the lofty but human view that her best work was never understood by the critics. She had, however, a more legitimate complaint, which R. C. Carton had already put forward; that plays were not judged on their own merit and intention, but by comparison with some other play of the moment which had caught the favour of the Press. I remember reading the damnation of what was meant to be the lightest of light comedies on the ground that it wasn't *Strife*. *Strife* was an intense drama by Galsworthy which Charles Frohman had produced during the Repertory Season at the Duke of York's Theatre which almost ruined him. He himself uttered the most subtle and true criticism of *Strife*. He gave the reason why its hold upon the playgoer must be slight when he said, "It's a play about strikes, not about a strike". But nothing would satisfy the dramatic critic of the day but *Strife*. Farcical comedies, historical tragedies, drawing-room melodramas, all must be swept away. In a succession of *Strifes* was to be seen the new dawn of the Drama.

During this year of 1900 Alexander had produced

and himself acted in four plays and had revived one
for eleven matinees: *Rupert of Hentzau, The Prisoner
of Zenda, The Man of Forty, A Debt of Honour*, and
The Wisdom of the Wise. Only one of these, *The
Man of Forty*, had reached one hundred performances, and that one only a hundred and two. Yet on
the year there was no loss. It may be interesting in
an age of soaring costs to look at the details in the
Profit and Loss Account of these plays.

Rupert of Hentzau had fifty-one performances.
Its share of the rent, rates, taxes, and insurance
amounted to £1064. The salaries paid to the company, £2253 : 17 : 4; to the staff in front of the House,
£477 : 7 : 9; the wages, including the stage hands,
came to £618 : 1 : 7. The wardrobe cost £143 : 16 : 2;
the orchestra £386 : 18 : 10; lighting was responsible
for £127 : 16 : 11, advertising and bill-posting for
£818 : 10 : 2, printing and stationery for £32 : 16 : 3.
The author's fees amounted to £429 : 16 : 5, those
of the auditors to £38 : 10 : 9, and miscellaneous
expenses to £77 : 14 : 1. Making thus a grand total
of £6470 : 6 : 3, or £126 : 17 : 4 and a fraction of
a penny a night. The takings, on the other hand,
came to £7701 : 1 : 6, a sum which was increased by
the rent of the bars to £7781 : 3 : 6. There was
therefore on the actual playing of the piece a profit of

$$
\begin{array}{rrr}
£7781 & 3 & 6 \\
-\ 6470 & 6 & 3 \\
\hline
£1310 & 17 & 3 \\
\end{array}
$$

But against this profit had to be put the cost of the
production, £1126 : 4 : 5; and half of the reopening

expenses after the tour, £184 : 12 : 10. Thus *Rupert of Hentzau* cancelled out.

The eleven matinees of *The Prisoner of Zenda* stand as follows. Rent, rates, etc., £226, artists' salaries £421 : 6 : 6, front of the house £70 : 7s., wages £86 : 3 : 1, wardrobe £25 : 10s., orchestra £89 : 9 : 2, lighting £25 : 9 : 1, advertising and bill-posting £180 : 2 : 7, printing and stationery £5 : 1 : 7, author's fees £86 : 8 : 1, auditors' £7 : 8s., miscell-aneous expenses £16 : 5 : 2=a total of £1246 : 10 : 3. The eleven matinees, however, brought in to the treasury £1727 : 19 : 6, increased by this play's share of the rent of the bars to £1744 : 17 : 6. There was thus a profit on playing of

$$
\begin{array}{rrr}
£1744 & 17 & 6 \\
- \ 1246 & 10 & 3 \\
\hline
£ \ 498 & 7 & 3 \\
\end{array}
$$

Against this profit had to be set a small cost of pro-duction, owing to renewals, etc., of £290 : 8 : 9, and half the reopening expenses after the tour, £184 : 12 : 10. The net result, therefore, on the eight weeks from February 1st to March 27th was a profit of £23 : 5 : 8.

The Man of Forty, produced the night after *Rupert of Hentzau* finished, ran for a hundred and two per-formances. The costs worked out: Rent, rates, taxes, insurance £2226 : 13 : 4, salaries of company £3094 : 10 : 10, of management and front staff £975 : 7s., wages £885 : 11 : 9, wardrobe £155 : 2 : 11, orchestra £672 : 8 : 3, lighting £193 : 14 : 5, adver-tising and bill-posting £1340 : 15 : 2, printing and stationery £100, author's fees £740 : 0 : 10, auditors' fees £74 : 16 : 3, miscellaneous £303 : 13 : 2 = a grand total of £10,762 : 14 : 10. The returns from the box office, on the other hand, were £12,743 : 13 : 6, increased by the rent of the bars £177, and royalties from the loan of opera-glasses £8 : 10 : 3, to £12,929 : 3 : 9. There was left, therefore, a profit on the playing of the piece for the fourteen weeks:

$$
\begin{array}{rrr}
£12,929 & 3 & 9 \\
-\quad 10,762 & 14 & 10 \\
\hline
£2,166 & 8 & 11 \\
\end{array}
$$

Against this profit is to be set the cost of production, which was not very high, £573 : 4 : 9. Deducting this sum from the profit on playing, we arrive at a net profit of £1593 : 4 : 2 on the completed run.

A Debt of Honour followed after the holiday season. Its total cost amounted to £8907 : 15 : 11, and it was acted eighty-five times, the receipts plus the rent of the bars and the royalties on the opera-glasses being £9946 : 15 : 2. On the playing, therefore, there was a credit balance of £1185 : 3 : 2. But most of that sum had already gone on the cost of production, and the net result was a profit of £174 : 9 : 4.

The Wisdom of the Wise brought the twelve months to an end. It enjoyed only fifty-four performances. Its cost was £5945 : 10 : 10 and it took £5144 : 9 : 2. There was a loss on the actual playing of £801 : 1 : 8. To this loss must be added the cost of the production, £1268 : 8 : 9, so the loss on the run of the play reached £2069 : 10 : 5.

There is no form of words which can make a successful season out of a sequence of four new plays, each one needing its preliminary advertisement, each one presented with the finish essential at the St. James' Theatre, and only one of them capable of lasting for a hundred nights. Even that imaginative Russian general who described himself in his despatch as advancing northwards when he was retreating from the Japanese, would be unequal to the requisite circumlocution. The year of 1900 was not a successful one for Alexander. Yet how did he stand at the end of the year's work? He had made, £23 : 5 : 8 out of *The Prisoner of Zenda* matinees, £1593 : 4 : 2 out of *A Man of Forty*, and £174 : 9 : 4 out of *A Debt of Honour* = £1790 : 19 : 2. He had lost on *The Wisdom of the Wise* £2069 : 10 : 5. He had therefore lost on the year £278 : 11 : 3. But besides being the manager of the theatre he was its leading actor, and as an actor drew a salary, not so large a salary as his abilities and the high esteem in which the public held him entitled him to draw, or as that which he received afterwards at Drury Lane, but a reasonable one. It amounted to £2558 : 6 : 8 and converted his loss into an earning of £2279 : 15 : 5. From this earning he made an outlay on plays for the future of £1249 : 10 : 5. And with the resulting sum of £1030 : 5s. he would have been left as the return for his year's activity, had he not established throughout the provinces a reputation for his touring companies. He sent out in August of 1900 a company playing *Rupert of Hentzau* and *The Prisoner of Zenda* to the smaller towns. This tour brought in a net profit of £473 : 12 : 5. He had shares in other touring companies, and especially in a tour of *Magda* with Mrs Patrick Campbell in the title-rôle which brought in a net profit of £1506 : 19 : 3. He hired out the scenery of *As You Like It* and sold some of the dresses for £207 : 9 : 9. So that at the end of an unsuccessful year he had laid out chiefly in the form of advances to authors £1249-odd, and had got besides £3217 and a few shillings.

It is worth while noticing in this summary of the year's doings that he could make a profit out of a play which ran less than ninety nights with the seats less than half filled and yet conduct his theatre with dignity and with a thoughtful consideration of its patrons.

The first play produced in 1901 did not improve the balance-sheet. Haddon Chambers' play *The Awakening* failed to arouse the slumbering playgoer, and it went itself to sleep after its sixtieth performance. However, a play by H. V. Esmond, *The Wilderness*, acted for the first time on April 11th, ran for fourteen weeks to houses of £170 a performance; and a very successful tour followed.

It was in keeping with that curious mixture of canniness and courage, prudence and audacity, which formed so large an element in Alexander's character that on this tour he should try out a revival of *The Importance of Being Earnest*. He had never had a doubt that a time would come, and within a reasonable period, when this iridescent bubble of gaiety and wit would dance in the air again to the delight of all men's ears and eyes. His only doubt was how

soon that time would come. He sought for an answer
to his riddle from the oracle of the provinces. If they
would take the brilliant comedy to their hearts,
washed clean of its associations by the passage of the
years, it would receive what it had not yet received,
its deserved recognition at the hands of the London
Press and public. Before, the man had eclipsed his
work. Alexander gave fourteen performances of the
play, but the oracle's answer was obscure, as is the
way with oracles. *The Importance of Being Earnest*
did better than *The Awakening*, a failure in London,
but not as well as those old warriors *The Idler* and
Liberty Hall, or his new play *The Wilderness*. Nevertheless he revived it in London early in the year
1902, announcing the revival "for a limited number
of performances". The revival was fairly successful.
The comedy ran for fifty-five nights to average
takings of £110 and, eked out with matinees of
Liberty Hall, kept the balance-sheet in order. But
the confederate season had clearly not yet come.

Meanwhile Alexander had been preparing an
ambitious enterprise. Some few years before he had
given a commission to Stephen Phillips, the author
of *Marpessa* and *Christ in Hades*, who wished to
write a poetic tragedy. He wrote *Paolo and Francesca* for Alexander. But the remodelling of the
theatre, the negotiations which had begun for a tour
in the United States, and the difficulty of securing
the star-cast which Alexander wanted, all hindered
the production. Meanwhile, of course, the advance
fees were renewed; Phillips had seen another play of
his, *Herod*, staged magnificently by Beerbohm Tree
at His Majesty's before large audiences, and had yet

a third play in rehearsal at the same theatre, a dramatisation of the *Odyssey* entitled *Ulysses*. Stephen Phillips, indeed, was, from the point of view of a dramatist, doing very well. But he was one of those people to whom even a large increase of income makes no difference. He lived obscurely in lodgings at Brighton or at a cottage at Ashford in Middlesex. He wrote his letters from a restaurant in East Street, Brighton, from the Marine Parade, from Great Yarmouth. But in spite of *Herod*, and *Ulysses*, and advances upon *Paolo and Francesca* there was always a need of money, or an acknowledgment of money received. For the rest he was the easiest author a manager could have to deal with, reasonable, ready to make and receive a suggestion and grateful for the efforts which Alexander was making to secure for the representation of the characters a cast of which London had never seen the like. To such a man Alexander was the most responsive of souls; and such a spirit of agreement and harmony was needed between them. For there were others, kindly, well-meaning people quite quite sure they were right, who were pulling Phillips this way and that way, casting his play for him, arranging his scenery, and bombarding the St. James' Theatre with advice.

Alexander's aim was to secure Mrs Patrick Campbell for Francesca, Dame Madge Kendal for Lucrezia and to play Giovanni Malatesta himself. Stephen Phillips, who had been irritated by some irresponsible suggestion in a newspaper that his play was to be postponed in favour of one by Clyde Fitch, was delighted. He wrote from Ashford in Middlesex.

DEAR ALEXANDER,

Mrs Campbell is of course *ideal.* Do make any effort in your power to get her. She would assure the success of the play from that peculiar glamour which is what the part wants. I should look forward to a long run if she will come. The proposal about Lucrezia is a stroke of genius which would never have occurred to me. Supposing these come off, and with yourself as Giovanni there remains only Paolo —for I leave Waller as still in doubt. I think on the whole Faber would be as good as any one. He leaves Tree very soon and goes elsewhere but no doubt could be got for January. What I feel about all these splendid possibilities is that as we have the advantage of a definite date—no depend-ence on the uncertainty of a run—it would be well to strike *at once* with these people so far as it is possible. . . . All my interests and hopes are now centred in your diplomacy— only do if possible press Mrs C. for a definite answer and agreement. . . ."

The dream, alas! dissolved into regrets—Stephen Phillips', Alexander's, and now, I think, the regrets of all lovers of the theatre. What a representation the tragedy would have had! The glamour of Mrs Patrick Campbell—Phillips used the right word to express her—the sympathy and tenderness of Dame Madge Kendal, Alexander splendidly striking out in a new and unexpected character—was Stephen Phillips not justified in hoping for "not merely an art success but a real great popular triumph"? But Mrs Patrick Campbell's help could not be obtained. Dame Madge Kendal was tempted but was debarred by the autumn tour of herself and her husband which had now become an annual institution. Alex-ander fell back upon Evelyn Millard for Francesca and Marie Brema for Lucrezia. Marie Brema, a *prima donna* of Covent Garden, had long preferred dramatic to operatic parts. Stephen Phillips was content. He had been thinking of Lena Ashwell, and Cissie Loftus, whom he had seen acting in *The Children of the King*, and Lily Brayton, but he had come to the conclusion that since Mrs Patrick Campbell's glamour was not to add to the play its haunting quality, "Miss Millard alone can play the part". The engagement of Marie Brema would take a weight off his mind.

But the two people who alone were really concerned in the affair, the author and the manager who was to produce it, were not left to themselves at all. There was an enthusiast in the background—one of the tremendous enthusiasts, greater than Trelawney, less than Forster, but busier than either of them: Sidney Colvin, the distinguished Librarian of the British Museum. No less enthusiastic was Mrs Colvin, his wife. It was the most genuine, overpowering enthusiasm that ever was known, and it had twice possessed them in the course of their lives; and on each occasion for someone alien from their ways. There was nothing Bohemian in the composition of Sidney Colvin. He was the courteous, cultured official, a little academic, almost a little prim. But the two men whose fortunes and fames he laboured to promote were Bohemians of the Latin Quarter. Robert Louis Stevenson, when asked by Andrew Lang to lunch with him at the Oxford and Cambridge Club, turned up to Lang's delight in a brigand's Inverness cape, a velvet coat, and a black-and-white striped shirt. Stephen Phillips was at his most comfortable in a public-house. And both these

men, in turn, by the greatness of their gifts took the
Colvins by storm. The Colvins worked for them,
even pestered for them. Colvin looked after Stevenson's business arrangements when that great writer
lived under the shadow of death in Samoa. He persuaded the Royal Academy to invite Phillips to
reply to the toast of Literature at its annual banquet,
and I should think Phillips is the only author who
ever turned that invitation down. But there came
with the enthusiasm a kind of jealousy, a sense of
proprietorship. The Colvins must be the only
advisers. Leave it to them and their blue-bird shall
soar—the world's kingfisher. *Paolo and Francesca*
was Phillips' finest work, limpid in its verse,
strong and simple in its action. Sidney Colvin
knew exactly how it ought to be cast, who should
be responsible for the scenery, how it should be
acted.

"Remember, I have never put my money on the
wrong horse yet in any of the arts", he wrote to
Alexander, when pressing for the engagement of a
young actress for Francesca.

He had discovered that young actress, or thought
he had. As a matter of fact she had already taken two
or three of the less important parts in plays at the St.
James' Theatre. She was Margaret Halstan. Sidney
Colvin went to see her, whether in a play or not he
does not say, and he found her "of the right poetical
appearance, strikingly handsome and radiant and at
the same time slender and girlish". He got her to
read the part of Francesca to him. She could express
poetry and passion. She was quick to make use of
criticisms. He carried her off to Stephen Phillips. She

read the part again to both of them. Sidney Colvin dashed off a letter to Alexander.

BRITISH MUSEUM

MY DEAR ALEXANDER, *July 6*

I want to tell you at once how much impressed both Phillips and I have been with Miss Halstan. I am quite sure she would make not only a thoroughly satisfactory but almost an ideal Francesca.

No one else would do. In most ways Margaret Halstan would be far better than Mrs Patrick Campbell. As for another suggested lady, her nose was too short for a heroine of romance; as for yet a third, she played modern comedy with a very pretty grace, pathos, and finish, but was not of the poetical cast and would be fatal to this play. Alexander meekly replied that he had engaged Margaret Halstan, and seems not to have explained that he had already with Stephen Phillips' entire agreement contracted that Evelyn Millard should play the part of Francesca. Margaret Halstan actually played the short but effective part of Tessa, the daughter of Pulci the drug-seller, and played it delightfully. One can read between the lines that when the truth came out poor Phillips was put in the corner for a bit. There had been, and I suppose as long as theatres exist often will be, a trifle of trouble over an inaccurate paragraph in this and that newspaper. Stephen Phillips wrote in haste and heat to Alexander, was reassured with a little acerbity, and replied contritely:

Believe me I should allow no one to come between you and me for a moment. Certain of my friends have made themselves rather disagreeable to me over the proposed casting of the play, but I stood to you as you know, and having agreed with you did not withdraw a step. Please don't imagine that I could, and rely on me in every way.

But Colvin was too sincere an enthusiast, too eager to see justice done to the poet and his work to sulk for more than five minutes. As he had helped others —Stevenson and Phillips were perhaps his chief debtors, but they were chiefs of a lengthy regiment —so he put all his great knowledge and all his judgment at the disposition of the St. James' Theatre. Telbin, the scene-painter, and E. V. Reynolds, the stage manager who could not only stage-manage but could give the most complete little miniature performances of the small character parts which his other duties allowed him to undertake, were both sent off to Italy. Colvin was anxious that the scenery and decorations should be characteristically thirteenth century and not Renaissance. They would find their best suggestions not at Rimini but in the architectural backgrounds to the frescoes of Cimabue and Giotto in the upper Church of Assisi, and in the old ruined *castello* of Assisi. Colvin might also be of use to Percy Macquoid "with some material for the period which may be new to him". He attended rehearsals, was soon reconciled to the Francesca of Evelyn Millard, and contributed some practical criticisms.

The very important part of Lucrezia was in the end taken by Elizabeth Robins, and H. R. Hignett made his London debut as Pulci, the old apothecary; Lilian Braithwaite was the Nita, a rather conventional figure who had stepped out of an eighteenth-century comedy of intrigue into blank verse; Arthur Machen represented Giovanni's servant; and a young and unknown actor borrowed from F. R. Benson's famous Shakespearian Company was brought up to London to play the ill-fated lover Paolo.

This last was no accidental engagement. A couple of years before, in a town of the North of England, Henry Ainley, a local amateur, had walked on, as the saying is, during the week of Alexander's engagement. He had sought Alexander's advice, since he was on fire to exchange the ledgers of a bank-clerk for the entrancing chances of the stage. Alexander, always a good and helpful judge of young actors, was quick to recognise Ainley's matchless aptitude for a theatrical career. But Ainley was a boy and his father looked upon the stage as the pit of Erebus. If Henry Ainley could persuade his father to let him go, something might be done. Ainley did in the end persuade his father, he was recommended to gain experience and flexibility of voice in the wide repertoire of Frank Benson; and from the first mooting of this play of *Paolo and Francesca* between Phillips and Alexander, Alexander carried in his mind the possibility that in this youth he was to find such a representation of Paolo as only a painter could imagine. He went down to Croydon where the Benson Company was acting, and after watching the performance of *The Merchant of Venice* in which Ainley played Lorenzo, he induced Benson to release him.

Henry Ainley had youth, grace, beauty of face, beauty of voice, and these native gifts won for him a popular success. But it was the success of a pet. Of the power and the command which were afterwards again and again to throw open to him the very throne-room of the actors' kingdom there was at present no real sign. There was a want of fire. He looked to be too spiritual. He was too tame. The passion, the resistance which sought in action the strength to continue to resist, the despair which looked for its reprieve in suicide, the final submission to an overwhelming love—for the vivid realisation of these emotions he was not yet ripe. There was a speech at the end of the second act where so swift and so clear a transition from argument to argument was needed as would have taxed the resources of Henry Irving himself. He had escaped:

> I have fled from her; have refused the rose,
> Although my brain was reeling at the scent.
> I have come hither as through pains of death;
> I have died, and I am gazing back at life.

Yet it was not too late to return. The white road to Rimini was still in view and at the end of it the towers upon the walls shone red with the setting of the sun:

> And might I not return? Those battlements
> Are burning. They catch fire, those parapets!
> And through the blaze doth her white face look out
> Like one forgot, yet possible to save.
> Might I not then return? Ah, no! no! no!
> For I should tremble to be touched by her,
> And dread the music of her mere good-night.
> Howe'er I sentinelled my bosom, yet
> That moment would arrive when instantly
> Our souls would flash together in one flame,
> And I should pour this torrent in her ear
> And suddenly catch her to my heart.

But at the moment when he is on the point of hurrying back, a drum is heard. His brother's soldiers, his command, are marching upon Florence. Paolo's salvation lies there:

> A drum!

It should be, of course, a loud cry ringing with hope:

> I'll lose her face in flashing brands, her voice
> In charging cries. . . .

But he stands stock-still whilst the soldiers march past him cheering him, their captain, calling upon him. He follows for a step or two. Then his old irresolution catches him up again:

> I cannot go; thrilling from Rimini,
> A tender voice makes all the trumpets mute.
> I cannot go from her: may not return.
> O God! what is Thy will upon me? Ah!
> One path there is, a straight path to the dark.
> There, in the ground, I can betray no more,
> And there for ever am I pure and cold.
> The means! No dagger blow, nor violence shown
> Upon my body to distress her eyes.
> Under some potion gently will I die;
> And they that find me dead shall lay me down
> Beautiful as a sleeper at her feet.

And upon that line the curtain descended. It was a dramatic scene and it taxed too strenuously the inexperience of the young actor. Emotional power was there—enough of it and to spare as after years from time to time disclosed. But it was locked up and Ainley had not yet found the key. It did not break through the screen of flesh, it was not audible in the level music of the voice. His *Paolo* was the Prince Charming of a fairy story, not the young living Italian with the hot sun in his blood.

The great performance, indeed, on that opening
night of March 6th, 1902, and on each of the hundred
and thirty-three performances which followed, was,
in the judgment of all the spectators, given by
George Alexander himself. The war-scarred im-
perious veteran who had married out of policy in
the grey of his life a girl from a convent; the man
"of savage courage and deliberate force" whose love
for his young brother was the one gentle element
in his nature—and there was a fierceness even in
that; this man bewildered, desperately hurt by the
sudden inrush of a tormenting passion for his child-
wife:

> How beautiful you seem, Francesca, now,
> As though new-risen with the bloom of dreams!
> More difficult it grows to leave your side.
> I, like a miser, run my fingers through
> Your hair: yet tears are lately in your eyes!
> What little grief perplexes you, my child?—

the veteran discovering that his beloved Paolo was
wooing her in his own despite, that his love was
returned by her, rushing in a frenzy of despair to a
squalid compounder of philtres; and in the end
driven on to kill the only two people who had lit up
his stormy and indefatigable life with tenderness:

> Now like a thief he creeps back to the house!
> To her for whom I had begun to long
> So late in life that now I may not cease
> From longing! . . .
> I will be wary of this creeping thing
> . . . And I am grown
> The accomplice and the instrument of Fate,
> A blade! A knife!—no more—

and when the deed was accomplished, speaking with
a simple dignity of despair:

> Carlo, go through the curtains, and pass in
> To the great sleeping-chamber: you shall find
> Two there together lying: place them, then,
> Upon some litter and have them hither brought
> With ceremony.   [*Exeunt* CARLO *and* FOUR SERVANTS.
>   GIOVANNI *paces to and fro.*
>   The curse, the curse of Cain!
> A restlessness has come into my blood,
> And I begin to wander from this hour
> Alone for evermore.
> LUC. (*rushing to him*): Giovanni, say
>   Quickly some light thing, lest we both go mad!
> GIO. Be still! A second wedding here begins,
>   And I would have all reverent and seemly:
>   For they were nobly born, and deep in love—

and moving to the litter where Paolo and Francesca
lie dead:

> Not easily have we three come to this—
> We three who now are dead. Unwillingly
> They loved, unwillingly I slew them. Now
> I kiss them on the forehead quietly.
>   [*He bends over the bodies and kisses them on the
>   forehead. He is shaken.*
> LUC. What ails you now?
> GIO.   She takes away my strength.
>   I did not know the dead could have such hair.
>   Hide them. They look like children fast asleep!

Giovanni Malatesta, tyrant of Rimini, required for
his portrayal an actor with a subtle grasp of character, a quiet intensity, and the grand manner of the
elder tragedians; an actor, made free by his experience and study and by his command of that necessary

GEORGE ALEXANDER
AS GIOVANNI IN *PAOLO AND FRANCESCA*

addition his own self and personality, to carry over the footlights into the consciousness of his audience the pitiful sense of a great man caught hopelessly in the nets of disaster. The drama no longer had its votaries with the life-histories of their favourite players at their fingers' ends. There were many present on that opening night who remembered George Alexander as the patient husband of Mrs Tanqueray, as the gay and high-spirited Rudolf Rassendyll, and as the irresistible Jack Worthing with his mourning suit, his black gloves, and his black-bordered handkerchief. But there were many too who were unfamiliar with the record of his years in the company of Sir Henry Irving. To them he was the *jeune premier* of the modern stage, fault-less in the fit of his clothes, nice in the adjustment of his cravat. To them the tormented figure of Giovanni Malatesta must have—nay did—come as a startling revelation. Those who had seen the char-acter grow from rehearsal to rehearsal were grateful rather than surprised. Addison Bright, the author and Phillips' agent, wrote:

A thousand thanks for a thing of great, great beauty which does you honour, and thanks again for the pleasure it has been to stand with you in however modest a way over something we can all be proud of. Nothing but glory can come of it, I'm sure; and for your own share in the shoulder-ing of the acting burden, nothing but a clamour of praise.

Sidney Colvin wrote:

Your performance struck me enormously, especially in Acts II and IV, and will give people quite a new idea of your powers.

And Stephen Phillips sent thanks:

From the bottom of my heart for the splendid courage and skill you have shown right through the whole production. . . . As to the artistic success there is luckily no need to speak of it—the general verdict being "the most beautiful production ever seen on the English stage". Personally, while I take great pride in all this, I am also sure that you yourself have made a very deep and real impression in Giovanni. People were growing only too accustomed to see you in a certain part, and now you have come out absolutely strong and big in a totally different way. So far then as I am concerned may I have the proud feeling that the play has been, to put it mildly, "good for you" and good for the theatre, which by this splendid production has taken a different position in the eyes of the world. I should like to feel this at any rate, as some return for all you have done for the play and myself. I only wish I could have been of more help but I was "done" when we rehearsed.

Paolo and Francesca, after a hundred and thirty-four memorable performances, ended with the season. Laurence Irving took it to the United States, but it secured there no more than a success of esteem. Nor has it since been revived in England. There was no relief to its doomfulness. The one scene with the soldiers at the inn on the road to Rimini which should have been light-hearted was written with too heavy a hand, and but for the beauty of the production and the acting it would hardly have held the boards as long as it did at the St. James'. Poetry, if it is to live, must be superlative. Essays, histories, fiction, may continue if they are very good or at times even if they are only good. We have it on the authority of Conrad that the turgid works of Bulwer

Lytton are to this day the favourite reading of the fo'c'sles of sailing-ships. But with poetry good and very good won't do. Who knows his Akenside? or Thomson's *Seasons?* or Dr. Young's *Night Thoughts?* Who acts in *Orinoko?* Phillips' best work —and without a doubt it is *Paolo and Francesca*— was poetry more human, more appealing, and had exquisite moments. But it ran in a narrow channel and it may well be that the brevity of its life was due in a measure to the hysteria of praise which acclaimed it. Phillips was raised to the company of Milton and Marlowe. He was the comet of his age. The laudations were too loud and he suffers now the penalty of too disdainful a neglect.

It was an odd habit of Alexander, when he came across a passage in a book which had a meaning for him, to have it printed and to carry it about with him in his pocket for a time. Here is one:

I have always taught, and do teach, and shall teach, I doubt not, till I die, that in resolving to do our work well is the only sound foundation of any religion whatever.

He was certainly following his precept out when he staged with so much beauty and care the play *Paolo and Francesca.*

CHAPTER IX

ON September 1st of that year 1902, Alexander
reopened the St. James' with a romantic drama
of France, written by Justin Huntly M'Carthy.
It was founded, no doubt, upon a legend which
Theodore de Banville had already used in a play of
one act. Here the story was expanded into four acts.
It was a suggestion developed, rather than a story
expanded, by a hand very adept at extracting
romance out of old stories. Alexander played François Villon the immortal rogue, Charles Fulton, an
actor with a deep voice, the superstitious old Louis
XI with the leaden medals dangling on his hat,
Henry Ainley played a small part, and Alfred Brydone,
and E. Lyall Swete, both distinguished recruits from
the Benson Company, represented the Provost of
Paris and the Grand Constable of France. Alexander
with his slim figure and picturesque appearance was
well suited to the period and the part. The play ran
for twenty-eight weeks and was succeeded on
March 19th in the following year, 1903, by one of
the few foreign plays produced during the life of
this management at the St. James' Theatre.

Old Heidelberg was a version by Rudolf Bleich-
mann of a German comedy *Alt Heidelberg*, of which

GEORGE ALEXANDER
AS FRANÇOIS VILLON IN *IF I WERE KING*

the author was Wilhelm Meyer-Forster. There are
two outstanding characters amongst the males of the
cast, Karl Heinrich the Hereditary Prince of Sachsen-
Karlsburg, one of those imaginary German princi-
palities which Stevenson's *Prince Otto* had placed
upon the map of literature if not of Europe, and Dr.
Jüttner, his tutor. Karl Heinrich was a lad in a pen
of red tape and ceremonies; Dr. Jüttner, an old and
bibulous scholar, cramped by the buckram of a
petty Court, and pining for the bright lights of his
old University. The enlargement of these two in the
free comradeship of Heidelberg, the one learning
youth for the first time, the other recapturing it; the
Prince's love-affair with the inn-keeper's daughter;
the old tutor's death in the midst of a party; the
Prince's return to his little capital to take up his little
sceptre, and the disillusionment which awaited him
when a year or two later he sought to revive amongst
his old club-fellows the spirit of their old conviviality
—made up a story which never fails to draw the easy
tear. The woes of Kings and Princes confined within
the heavy decorum of a Court are always pleasant
spectacles for the commoner. "How lucky I am",
he says on his way home to Surbiton. "I have only
one paper to sign to-morrow." And though the
paper be the cheque for his income-tax he signs it
with the less displeasure.

It was Alexander's intention to play the part of
the tutor Dr. Jüttner in this production. There was
more vivacity in it, more opportunity for the actor
in this rejuvenescence of an old man in the company
of the young and in the underlying sense of shame it
brought with it. But the Home-Front was mobilised

against him at once. He resisted stoutly, and under swift direction from the Home-Front a flank attack, the attack of a Gallieni at the Marne, was organised by the theatre staff. Lady Alexander flew down to the theatre and gathered them together, C. T. H. Helmsley the business-manager, Whittaker and Horne the secretaries, Arnold of the box office, E. V. Reynolds the stage-manager. "Chief, you can't do that! You must play Karl Heinrich!"

Alexander went home to Pont Street: "They're all mad at the theatre", he cried. "I'm over forty."

"But you don't look it, my dear", said Mrs Alexander.

"They're very experienced people and perhaps they're right."

Right or wrong, she had her way. J. D. Beveridge was cast for the part of Dr. Jüttner and gave an admirable performance. Alexander played Karl Heinrich, with the exception of the interval of a fourteen-weeks' tour, until the middle of March in the following year; and though he was then in his forty-fifth year, he carried off this picture of student life without a sign of maturity. Sir Francis Jeune wrote to him on the day following the *première*:

My DEAR ALEXANDER,

I must send you my heartiest thanks and congratulations for the delightful play of last night. I confess I felt nervous for I had doubts whether the German Play was substantial enough to hold an English audience. But you conquered all difficulties—and certainly one of the greatest causes of the very remarkable success of the play was your own wonderful impersonation of the youthful, or rather boyish, Karl. And the acting was certainly excellent throughout.

GEORGE ALEXANDER
AS KARL HEINRICH IN *OLD HEIDELBERG*

During the autumn of 1905 Alexander acted for the first time in fifteen years under a management other than his own. The copious pen of Hall Caine had been used to adapt for the stage a novel of his, *The Prodigal Son*. Arthur Collins had accepted it for the autumn production at Drury Lane. Both he and Hall Caine were anxious to secure Alexander for the principal part. He had, as he so often did when he was away upon his tour, let the St. James' Theatre to the Kendals, and he had pencilled in, as the technical phrase goes, a lengthy tour of the British Isles. But such arrangements were not so very difficult to cancel. Promises could be made for the future. Arthur Collins could lend his help in agreeing to send his Drury Lane drama to those provincial theatres which released Alexander. Alexander himself would be spared the fatigue and anxiety inseparable from a tour with a large company and a great load of costly scenery; and the salary which he was offered was within £1000 of the net profit which he might expect to make after all his travelling. He agreed, therefore, to go to Drury Lane at the salary of £250 a week, the total sum to be not less than £3500. In other words, fourteen weeks' pay was guaranteed to him. Nevertheless it must have needed more than a little courage for a man so firmly established in his own theatre to risk an adventure in the strange and vast environment of Drury Lane. But want of courage was never one of his vices. He may have been attracted by the names of the famous men who had stridden those boards. Certainly Arthur Collins plied him with them. He may have found it amusing once more to act with no responsibility but his part. He went at all events to the Lane and played in *The Prodigal Son*. The piece was one of those flamboyant emotional melodramas, requiring crowds and large scenes, which were the speciality of Greeba Castle, and with Alexander's help—not only as an actor, for he took a hand in the production—it ran easily during the appointed time.

It was as well that he was in London that autumn. For a few minutes before midnight of Friday, October 13th, his old chief, Sir Henry Irving, died in the hall of his hotel at Bradford. The body was brought to London on Saturday night and taken to his flat at 17 Stratton Street. At a meeting held on the Monday at the Hyde Park Hotel, George Alexander and Norman Forbes-Robertson were appointed as honorary secretaries to make the necessary arrangements for the funeral, which by the consent of the Dean, Dr. Armytage Robinson, was to take place at Westminster Abbey.

It is understood that Sir Anderson Critchett, the famous oculist, was chiefly instrumental in obtaining the Dean's consent; and a curious and rather grotesque story is told and vouched for. Sir Anderson himself, a devotee of the theatre and a brother of R. C. Carton the dramatist, had recently operated with success upon the Dean's eyes. Armytage Robinson, a great scholar, had been distressed beyond measure by the prospect of blindness, and in his gratitude promised Critchett that he would make him any return which he possibly could. Irving's friends approached Critchett to help them. The Dean and Chapter of St. Paul's had refused to allow the great actor's interment in their Cathedral. Would Dean Armytage Robinson consent to allow the precedent of Garrick to be repeated at Westminster Abbey? It was known that the Dean's sister, who had great influence with him, was violently opposed to any such ceremony. The Dean, however, was in bed in a dark room, though with his sister in attendance. Critchett consented to use his influence, and whilst the chief amongst Irving's friends waited in a room apart, Critchett penetrated into the darkened bedroom. He was greeted by a feminine voice from the gloom. "No! No actors!" But stout of heart he approached the bed, and reminding the Dean of his promise, appealed for the burial in the Abbey. But the voice from the shadows punctuated his every sentence. "No actors! No actors!" The Dean, however, stood by his promise, and Critchett coming out, informed Irving's old friends and managers that the Dean's consent had been given. So great was the relief felt by them that more than one burst into tears. The arrangements were made with all that care for detail which was natural to Alexander. He owed much to Irving—his debut in London, his regular and steady employment—and though no doubt he felt from time to time, as all in that company did, the sharp edge of their chief's stinging tongue, he was none the worse for it. A great kindness existed between the two men, and Alexander paid what he could of his debt in the perfect ordering of those last rites.

He returned to the St. James' Theatre in January of 1906 to enter upon the best two years of his career.

§

It will be remembered that after the production
of *The Princess and the Butterfly* Pinero refused in
the most unhesitating terms to contemplate any
future co-operation with the manager of the St.
James' Theatre. Two dictators in one playhouse at
the same time were equal to one ordeal of misery
which no sensible man would be willing to accept
for a second time. Quarrels on the stage, however,
are, as a rule, as frequent and as short-lived as stage
quarrels. The actor's life promotes them. His work
cannot be done in solitude, or with the help of a staff
which has only his interests to serve. It is done in
conjunction with other actors who have other interests at heart. Each being human is inclined to
think that by making the most of his individual
merits he is best serving the general cause. Hence
come violent clashes and fervid reconciliations.
Moreover, a kind of nervousness and sensibility
seem inseparable from the actor's calling, and show
themselves in an exaggeration of trivialities. A storm
in a teacup is easily magnified into a tornado in the
Atlantic. An omission due to forgetfulness becomes
an intended slight and a small success an achievement which the world will never forget. There is an
actress who dates every event in the stirring history
of the last thirty years backwards and forwards from
the time when she sang her one song at the Gaiety.
The date of the Coronation? Oh yes, that was so
many years after *The Soldiers on the Green*. In this
quarrel, however, it was the actor who did not
exaggerate and waited his time.

It came in 1904. On October 12th of that year, a play by Pinero entitled *The Wife without a Smile* was produced at Wyndham's Theatre. Why he wrote it will probably always remain a puzzle. It was not of course the first time that a distinguished author has suddenly run riot and lent his talents and his name to an eccentricity. *The Wife without a Smile* was a vagary, but a vagary which did its author a vast amount of harm. It threatened him with disrepute. It was received by the Press with unmitigated condemnation, and although for a few weeks it attracted to Wyndham's Theatre the sort of audience which is tickled by a salacity, it collapsed altogether very shortly afterwards.

Some time during that autumn I met Alexander one morning when we were riding in the Row. He told me that before the withdrawal of *The Wife without a Smile*—at the moment in fact when Pinero was the object of all the shafts of vituperative criticism—he had approached Pinero with a request that he should write another play for the St. James'. It was more than a request, it was an urgent plea. Alexander was always concerned with the status of the stage. The stage was his profession, he was proud of it, proud of the high position he had attained upon it, and he was never guilty of the silly snobbishness which treats it as a side-line. The only letters which he ever wrote to the Press were written to repel some hasty reflection which seemed to diminish its dignity. Criticism of himself was in the day's work and he took it with equanimity. But utter a slur upon the stage as a social institution and he flew to the defence of it. The high repute which it had acquired by the work of Henry Irving and the Bancrofts, and which the Kendals, and John Hare and Beerbohm Tree and the authors who wrote for them had sustained, was not to be impaired if he could help it. He was convinced now that if Pinero lost his high position amongst the dramatists, the status of the stage would be inevitably lowered. He discoursed earnestly to me under the trees as we walked our horses along the rails. Pinero brought to his work not only a supreme knowledge of the conditions under which a dramatist must work, but an intellectual equipment and a courage which few others possessed. The joke and the clever twist which falsified all the characters in order to bring down the curtain upon a comfortable conclusion were devices foreign to Pinero, impossible to him. He might have perpetrated a vagary. But you must not forget on that account the work which had gone before. It had an integrity and an aim which were not to be denied. Alexander had therefore put his theatre at Pinero's disposal. His next play, and as soon as possible, his own subject, his own conditions! Pinero was willing, and through the year 1905 he worked at *His House in Order*. By July he was sufficiently advanced to write about the cast. Would "kind Mrs Alec" go and see a certain lady? "Swete and Lowne—good." He regretted that Iris Hawkins could not be got to play the boy Derek Jesson. He wanted a real Frenchwoman for the governess Mademoiselle Thomé.

Miss —— speaks French perfectly but, when it comes to broken English, that is an obvious assumption. No one can give you natural broken English but a foreigner. Forgive me if I have inconvenienced you in this matter. You could keep a hold on Miss —— as a second string, but I should like you to find a handsome French lady of about 30.

In the month of September the play was getting on, but Pinero was still troubled about the difficulty of getting Derek Jesson properly acted. He wrote on the 22nd of that month:

MY DEAR ALEC,

Yes, the character is that of a boy—"a serious, wise-looking child of delicate physique". He is eight years old. I doubt whether you could find a real boy to look it and do it. A girl is, as a rule, so much the more graceful, charming and receptive. A comic boy is to be got, but hardly the other sort. However, if you can put your hand upon the prodigy, Barkis "is willing".

The dates you give me in your letter are most attractive. But can it be managed? You ask me if I have finished. Cruel! Heartless! Have I ever finished till about ten minutes before the first rehearsal? The position of affairs is this. Acts I and II go to the printers on Monday. Act III I am now engaged upon; and then there is Act IV to follow. . . .

It would indeed be delightful if we could get the earlier production you propose and, once more, I assure you I will do all in my power to aid your altered plans.

Yours ever,

ARTHUR W. PINERO

P.S.—I do hope you won't be disappointed at the, apparent, simplicity of the play.

Pinero was, you will observe, altogether charming and amenable. On October 12th he was able to write:

MY DEAR ALEC,

Here is the proof of the print of Acts I and II. I wish I could have sent you Act III—which is progressing famously—at the same time, so that you could have seen at the first glance how every hint and every clue contained in the earlier acts are followed up and rounded off. However, I shall not, I think, keep you long without the concluding portions of the piece.

I hope you won't allow yourself, at this stage, to be very seriously disappointed with the character of Hilary Jesson—who, necessarily, has to play somewhat of a waiting game.

He received a telegram and a letter by return of post. Here is the letter:

My dear Pin,

The first two acts are all I expected them to be—life-like and interesting from beginning to end. True comedy. Hilary could not be better or different in the earlier part of the play. It would be a great comfort to be able to begin rehearsals on the 1st of December at latest and to do the play early in January. Perhaps you will be able to say "yes" to this during the next month.

Yours,

Alec

P.S.—I shall make no definite plans for any play until we meet.

Pinero answered on the next day:

I need not tell you how pleased I am that you are satisfied with the work so far as it is in your hands.

I think there is no doubt that we shall be able to begin rehearsing on December 1st. Even if the last act is not by that time through the press, the three other acts will fully occupy us till it is.

No words could have convinced Alexander more completely that the play was smoothing out to its conclusion than Pinero's willingness to fix a date for

the first rehearsal before the last act was written.
Herbert Waring had been suggested for Filmer
Jesson, the too methodical and tidy Member of
Parliament. There was in all the stage-work which
Herbert Waring ever did, a curious touch of the
pedantic—something in his voice, his walk, his very
gestures—which made him more suitable to that
character than any other living actor. C. M. Lowne,
who played in so many of Pinero's plays, was marked
out for Pryce Ridgeley. As no one could better
represent the unromantic lover, the middle-aged man
with a tender heart carefully secluded from the
public gaze, so no one could be more utterly in-
sufferable when required so to be. I have vivid recollections of him in *Lady Frederick* as he described
the dinner which he had enjoyed in the Riviera
Express and again in the charming scene which ended
that first comedy of Somerset Maugham. But in
His House in Order, so completely did he identify
himself with that superior prig Pryce Ridgeley, that
one itched to inflict upon him in the words of Wilde's
Lady Bracknell "the worst excesses of the French
Revolution".

Pinero was still troubled over the boy Derek
Jesson:

You have seen, of course [he wrote], with your keen eye,
the importance of the *child*—an importance which does not
lessen as the play proceeds. Iris Hawkins would, I suppose,
be the *best*; but if she is not available, and you know of no
one in particular, Boucicault might help us. If we could find a
child *as clever as little Hawkins*, the novelty might be better
for us.

I have asked Lowne to write you again.

Would Nigel Playfair do for Dilnott? . . . A handsome, *real* French lady would be the ticket for Mlle. Thomé, don't you agree with me. It would give just the right touch to the thing.

In the end Arthur Bourchier released Iris Hawkins from her engagement to him and she played the boy with just that brutality which the part demanded.

The rehearsals on this occasion were conducted on both sides with a watchful cordiality. The company to interpret the play had been Pinero's choice and it was above all intelligent. It was quick to take up a suggestion and translate it into action. Irene Vanbrugh, who played the extremely important part of Nina Jesson, knew the author well from other plays and what he wanted. No Pinero play was complete without Lowne, so Lowne was there. Pinero had the French woman whom he had clamoured for, the child, a free hand in the direction—everything. Alexander was nursing him—meek as a lamb. After a rehearsal on a Friday he went home to Pont Street and wrote:

My dear Pin,

Thank you for your kind words to-day, I know I am a disappointment at rehearsal and that you are very patient and sympathetic. I think that you will find that I shall serve you better than you imagine. Talk to me quite freely, and I will do my best to be worthy of your trust. Only don't lose confidence in me.

Yours ever,
Alec

Pinero replied in the same strain. The spirit of the

millennium brooded above the roof of the St. James'
Theatre:

I am glad to receive your kind note because it gives me
the opportunity of saying, more expressly than I have been
able to say hitherto, that I have *every* confidence in your
ability to deal successfully, and brilliantly, with your very
difficult task. My anxiety that you should do yourself the
fullest justice in a part which is a little foreign to your usual
methods may show itself too strongly; but you will not
blame me in your heart for this. Once more, Alec—I look
to you to pull us through, and I feel sure I shall not be
disappointed.

No, it is not you, but one or two other things that worry
me—unnecessarily, you may think. The tone of our library,
in particular, mocks at me in my sleepless hours. This scene
was to have been our touch of the picturesque—"the old
part of the building"—and Mr Macquoid has given us a bit
of brand-new Shoolbred. It is this apartment that was to
have conveyed the idea that Annabel's boudoir was also an
old room. How else could the dry-rotten boards of her
cupboard have been so easily removable? But perhaps you
will tell me I fret about trifles. Do, if you can—for my
consolation.

The drawing-room is perfect—just what I imagined, and
the hall will be good when finished off. Get an important bit
of furniture to face the fireplace, if you can put your hand
readily on such a thing.

Again, God bless you and send you luck.

Yours always,

P.

It was, indeed, a crucial moment in the fortunes
of Pinero, and Alexander had been well inspired
when he persuaded him to return to the St. James'.

The play, although not perhaps on the plane of *Iris*, must stand high in any estimation of its author's work. There was less sign of effort in the dialogue. There was only one sentence which was discomforting. The comedy never dropped into farce. The story was fresh if not new. It was satire without caricature, and drama without exaggeration. And the play was by far the greatest success which Alexander had in all the twenty-five years of his management, or Pinero in his long life as an author.

His House in Order ran continuously for fifty-seven weeks, from January 31st, 1906, to February 27th, 1907. Four hundred and twenty-seven performances were given and the receipts amounted to £78,189 : 12s. The net profit reached £23,443. And at the final audit of the play in 1910, taking in Alexander's salary as actor, the profits on his own tours and on his provincial companies, it had brought in a total earning of £36,638 : 15 : 4.

CHAPTER X

HIS HOUSE IN ORDER was followed by Alfred
Sutro's *John Glayde's Honour*. And that by a translation of Bernstein's *Le Voleur*. The two plays between them, with a six-weeks' tour of *His House in
Order*, filled up a year and increased the prosperity
of the theatre. It is a proof of the sagacity with which
the St. James' was managed that *John Glayde's
Honour*, with no more than a hundred and thirty-
eight performances, brought in a net profit of over
£4750. The scene was set in Paris, the characters
were modish. The play required effective scenery
and beautiful clothes. Yet on a run so ordinary so
great a benefit could be obtained. The explanation
is that Alexander was quick to understand when a
play was sagging because of one of those temporary
depressions which once or twice or even more often
in any year afflict the theatres of London, or whether
it was dying. If it was dying he was no less quick to
whip it off before its vitality was quite exhausted.
It was a characteristic of the Grand Panjandrum that
the gunpowder ran out of the heels of his boots.
That is nothing to the money which runs out of a
theatre when a play is kept on after its popularity has
gone. But Alexander had always old plays and their

scenery and their dresses, and they could be revived at the shortest notice. *Lady Windermere's Fan*, for instance, was put on at the end of 1904 when *The Garden of Lies* had failed, and was continued for twelve weeks to a considerable gain.

Thus life was a smooth, busy, and prosperous affair for the Alexanders. The staff at the theatre was able and devoted. When plays lost money, they lost very little, and when they gained, they gained much. The Alexanders had moved to Pont Street during the run of *The Triumph of the Philistines* in the spring of 1895. They had room in their present house to entertain their friends. At times, some commodious place like the big reception rooms and terrace of the Royal Automobile Club would be taken for a big party during the season, and summer holidays would be spent in the Scottish Highlands. They both took an active part in the charities of their profession; and in the multifarious duties which distinction entails.

Alexander at the end of 1906 was forty-eight years old and his thoughts and ambitions were taking a new direction. At one time he had it in his mind to put some other actor into the St. James' as its protagonist and to confine himself to running it as a business. At another he thought of letting it go altogether. His own hopes were beginning to be set on public service.

He was chosen to stand in South St. Pancras for the Moderate Party at the L.C.C. election in March 1907. His fellow candidate was Mr Frank Goldsmith. At the previous election of 1904 the Progressive Socialist candidates had been George

Bernard Shaw and Sir William Geary, Baronet—a combination which produced some lighter moments during the contest. George Bernard Shaw sent his portrait to the electors but omitted to enclose a polling-card. Whether the combination or the omission affected the result, the two seats were lost, to the Progressive Socialists. At the 1907 election, Major Gastrell retired and George Alexander stood for the seat which he had held. The other Moderate candidate was again Frank Goldsmith.

It will be remembered that at the Parliamentary election in January of that year, the Liberals had swept the field. The Conservative Party received a shattering blow from which it took fifteen years to recover. In the House of Commons it could muster only a section where before it had paraded a battalion. The hopes of the Progressive Socialists that they would retain in the London County Council the power which they had held for the eighteen years of the Council's existence were naturally confident and high. But other important conditions were being left out of the reckoning. The Parliamentary election had been fought chiefly upon the outstanding question of Tariff Reform. The secondary contention was the use of Chinese Labour in the gold-fields of South Africa. On this latter problem there is now general agreement that the Liberal objection to it was wise and in a strict harmony with the later traditions of the race. But at the time both these problems were strongly felt and hotly discussed. They cut clean across the ordinary divisions of Conservative and Liberal, and many a staunch Conservative helped to put a Liberal in because first he was a free-trader, as the phrase went, and secondly because there was still magic in the name of Wilberforce. Clapham and Manchester between them disposed of the Conservative Party for the longer part of a generation.

But these two grave questions were the concern of the Imperial Parliament and of the Imperial Parliament alone. They did not enter into Municipal politics. No conclusion that a similar triumph awaited the Progressive Socialists at the County Council Election in March could prudently be drawn. In fact the Government in Parliament had as a rule worn a different colour from that of the Government in the London County Council. Moreover there were now a great number of young Conservatives with some experience of and still more enthusiasm for public life, who were put out of a job by the election. The General Election was fought in January 1907. The defeated candidates were free in March and the London County Council was their opportunity. The present Secretary of State for Foreign Affairs Samuel Hoare, Frederick Hall, Walter Guinness, Rupert Guinness, Montague Barlow, Felix Cassel, William Peel—they all seem to be knights or baronets or earls nowadays, and a handsome percentage of them has held or is holding the high offices of State—with political barristers and business men and women who wanted nothing more than to serve the county of London, flung themselves into this contest. The hoardings of the town became colourful with the picture of a Progressive Socialist smoking a big cigar and saying "It's your money we want". For once the civic conscience of the Londoner was stirred into activity. He actually went to the poll. Yes, on his way to, or his way home from, work, or in his luncheon hour, he did actually vote. The majority which had lasted through eighteen years was dissolved. The Moderates were for the first time in power.

The opponents of George Alexander and Frank Goldsmith in South St. Pancras were the Rev. Silvester Horne, a famous pastor of Whitefield's Tabernacle in the Tottenham Court Road, and his colleague in the pastorate; but they were beaten by a large majority. Bernard Shaw's comment was, "They were beaten by the Comedian and the Jew". Alexander brought to his new duties the studious care which he had given to his theatre. He served on the Highways, Rivers, Public Health, Midwives Act, and Parliamentary Committees during his six-years' membership of the Council; and during the five years from 1908 to 1912 he was continuously on the Parks and Open Spaces Committee. He became chairman of that body in March 1909 and continued to preside over it until March 1910, and in the opinion of some who served with him proved the most efficient chairman which that Committee had up till then had, in ensuring both the thoroughness of its work and the speed with which it was conducted.

Nor did he spare himself in the general business of the County Council. A suave and polished speaker, he was very useful when passion was rising. He spoke on the feeding of school-children and the care of crippled children, and took an infinity of trouble that what he said should be founded upon know-ledge. His notes written in pencil remain, and the manuscripts of speeches written out and corrected and corrected again. Meanwhile he gave his attention and his presence to the needs of South St. Pancras. There were social functions to be attended, philanthropic efforts to be supported, and in all these matters of importance to a constituency his wife lent her tireless help.

Meanwhile he was acting eight times a week and producing plays. His plans for the future disposition of his theatre were still in abeyance. The necessity for a decision was not imminent. He could combine the activities of a member of the County Council with the direction of a theatre, even though from time to time when the curtain fell he must hurry back to Spring Gardens for an all-night sitting.

But he was looking now towards the larger opportunity—a Parliamentary constituency in London. In London it must be, if it was to be at all; for in London he was known as a successful man of affairs as well as an actor. The Central Offices of the Conservative Association, however, were true to the spirit and method of all Political Associations. Show them a likely man and they will waste him if they can. Alexander was invited to contest Battersea against John Burns at the next General Election. There was never a hope, of course, that that seat could be won. John Burns was entrenched in Battersea, had been entrenched there for years; and he had now the added prestige which belongs to a Cabinet Minister. He lived in his constituency. He had justified his appointment to his Office by his command of it. He was a good fighter, he was liked by his opponents as by his supporters, and he had the invaluable backing of a general recognition that his right place was in the House of Commons. The most that an opponent could hope to do would be to keep him busy in his own constituency whilst the election was being fought. It was the task for some young and eager bantam who wanted to establish a claim upon his Party by putting up a fine fight in a hopeless cause, and could afford to wait. For a man who had made his own way to an established prosperity through the chances of a profession as precarious as any that exists in the world, who was proving at South St. Pancras that the courage and judgment which he had shown in the conduct of his private life were at his service too in his public life; for such an one a better chance of success must be the condition on which he stood. He must win a seat, no doubt. A novice, except he possess some knowledge or aptitude at that moment particularly valuable or a great local reputation, must expect no less. But a man over fifty years of age, as Alexander would be when the next General Election came, must fight for a seat which can be won or leave Parliament alone. Whether Alexander would ever have allowed himself to be lured by Percival Hughes into so hopeless an adventure as Battersea, I cannot say. It is unlikely. But he had a warm and shrewd friend in the Duke of Fife; and the Duke of Fife strongly advised him to decline the proposition. During the course of that Parliament, C. A. Whitmore, a most respected and diligent Member of the House of Commons who had long represented the borough of Chelsea, died and Lord Farquhar supported a suggestion that Alexander should take his place. But it came to nothing.

Later on Walworth was proposed, and Alexander went as far as to pay £150 towards the registration expenses which that borough's Conservative Association urgently demanded as a preliminary to the selection of a prospective candidate. But by that time Alexander's health was undermined by the malady of diabetes. Insulin was not yet discovered. Alleviations were empirical. There was no cure. Alexander abandoned his project and in 1912 he decided not to stand again for the London County Council. He had represented his constituency for six years and he received, when his determination was known, many expressions of regret. Thus Captain H. M. Jessel (now Lord Jessel), then Member of Parliament for the borough of South St. Pancras, wrote:

I am positive that the news of your intention not to stand again will be received with regret and dismay by all your friends and their number is legion in South St. Pancras. You and Lady Alexander have done so much in every way that you will both leave a void not only in the political but in the social life which it will be almost impossible to fill.

Personally, I am exceedingly sorry, as our relations have always been so pleasant. I, however, quite realise your reasons and, after all, considerations of health are paramount. You have, however, splendidly fulfilled your civic duty and set an example from a busy life to others who are only too prone to forget their duties and too ready to criticise.

Captain Swinton, who then led the Moderate Party in the London County Council, wrote in the same spirit, whilst the Executive Committee of the South St. Pancras Unionist and Conservative Association passed by a unanimous vote the following cordial resolution:

"That this meeting of the Executive Committee of the South St. Pancras Unionist and Conservative Association learns with profound regret that it is not the intention of Sir George Alexander to offer himself again as a candidate for the London County Council at the forthcoming election. They desire to place on record their high appreciation of the efficient manner in which he has fulfilled his duties as one of the representatives of S. St. Pancras during the past years, and the eminent services he has rendered not only to the division but to the whole of London during that period.

"They desire also to thank Lady Alexander for the kind interest and support she has given to all local matters during that period, and hope that they may both still be seen amongst the ratepayers in the division who cannot afford to lose such excellent friends."

It is pleasant also to be able to record that, upon his death, the Liberal and Radical Association sent to Lady Alexander a message of the deepest sympathy and a hope that her grief might be assuaged by the knowledge that her husband had been much esteemed by all who knew him in St. Pancras.

§

During the Coronation year of 1911, Alexander received the honour of a knighthood. The telegrams and letters which poured in upon him and Lady Alexander must have taken weeks of solid work to answer. The list of famous names attached to them would fill pages. Old friends, new friends, friends unknown sent their congratulations and bore witness to the pleasure which they felt. I quote only two; one from a young lady of New Malden which is too delicious to need any comment:

When I saw in the paper the other day that you had been made "Sir" Alexander, I nearly went mad in my excitement, for I am an awful tomboy. I do love your acting so, I think you are streets ahead of Lewis Waller, although some people do not think so. I have been to see you heaps of times, and I would come every day if I could.

The other from Sir Laurence Gomme, the secretary to the London County Council, will have been appreciated by Alexander and his wife for another reason than unconscious humour. It speaks sufficiently for itself, and fitly ends this short chapter on the share which he took in the public life of the County of London.

Dear Sir George Alexander,

You will permit me to offer my sincerest congratulations upon your distinction. To those of us who believe in the drama as one of the best means of educating people to a sense of beauty and proportion this compliment to you comes very closely home. Please ask Lady Alexander to allow me to include her in my congratulations and I am sure the whole staff at Spring Gardens feel glad that such a distinction should have come to so distinguished a member of the Council.

Yours very truly,
Laurence Gomme

Perhaps, however, there is a still more fitting end in a moving letter which Alexander himself wrote

GEORGE ALEXANDER WITH HIS DOGS

in answer to Pinero's congratulations. These two men had been, in spite of quarrels and disagreements, the moving spirits in the enlargement of the theatre; and whatever good work either of them did, in the best of it they were linked together. Alexander's letter was written at Pont Street on June 26th, 1911:

My dear Pin,

Your letter is dated 21st June. I ought to have answered it sooner. I have written to many friends, but I find it difficult to say what my heart dictates, to you. I am deeply sensible of how much gratitude I owe to your "written words"—you have enabled me to win distinction, and money too, and these two things mean a lot in our short lives. That my good luck is *pleasant* to you is a *delight* to me and my wife and I send you our dear love, and every token of a sincere regard.

Yours affly.

George Alexander

CHAPTER XI

DURING the years of his Municipal service Alexander produced two more plays by Sir Arthur Pinero—*The Thunderbolt* and *Mid-Channel*. Both of them were acted exactly fifty-eight times, so that each of them meant a loss of a moderate kind. But there was no other similarity between them. *The Thunderbolt* was a play about a sordid family squabble over a will which had disappeared. The characters were, with one exception, inhabitants of a small town, greedy, jealous, with a fallacious assumption of prosperity which at all costs they must keep up—characters, in fact, by Henry Arthur Jones. Amongst them stood the illegitimate daughter of the dead man, a girl who was more distressed by the idea that her father had shown so little love for her than by the loss of his fortune. *The Thunderbolt* was the confession of one of the family, a poor music-master, that his wife had destroyed the missing will. It was not, to be frank about it, a sufficiently interesting story. The subject was the sort of subject which Balzac might have seized upon, and out of its very sordidness and squalor extracted some grim and uncompromising picture of triumphant greed. For the greedy would have triumphed in the Balzac

192

story, the daughter would have been thrown out to fend for herself as best she could. She would have failed as an artist and sunk to the gutter, whilst the greedy would have ended in a blaze of provincial glory, mayors and aldermen and councillors without a qualm of self-reproach to trouble the gross contentment of their bellies. But the personages in *The Thunderbolt* were too weakly a lot, the girl who was to be their contrast was too colourless; and for once in a way the play at the St. James' was not satisfactorily cast.

Mid-Channel, on the other hand, ranks with *Iris*, or next to *Iris*, as the most sincere and acute piece of analysis which Pinero gave to the theatre. It did not depend upon the social conditions of the moment which within the passage of a lustrum may make your work old-fashioned. It did not pivot round a since-discarded theory as *The Doctor's Dilemma* pivoted about the opsonin test. It was a truth in any age. Pinero used in order to expound his theme, a trope for which he had a great partiality. Between Dover and Folkestone and the French coast stretches a shoal, Le Colbart, or The Ridge. Pinero places it in mid-Channel although the Varne shoal is a mile or so nearer to the centre of the passage. But both are noticeable for strong ripples both at spring tides and neaps even when the weather is fine, and if the wind be against the tide or the weather stormy, both will be boiling with breaking seas. Between the Channel passage and matrimony the commentator in the play—Peter Mottram, a character acted by C. M. Lowne—draws his parallel. Half-way across, there will be discomfort, dislike of one's fellow passengers, a perception of their faults and of the blemishes in their appearance, an inability to endure them. Half-way through married life is half-way across the Channel. The discomfort will be the matter of a few minutes, so long as the passengers understand that they are on the Ridge, that they are in mid-Channel, that in a few minutes their ship will get steady again and their discomfort vanish. The play is the dramatic analysis of two who did not understand. There is some admirable comedy and some lines as amusing as Pinero ever wrote. Mrs Annerly's statement for instance: "And Goodness knows I've no ambition to appear in the Divorce Court again—I hate the hole". But the play was a tragedy, and its author shirked nothing which could heighten its poignancy. It ended in suicide. One can say that it began to end in suicide in the very first scene.

"You'll see", says Zoe, the woman of the marriage, "when I put an end to myself, it will be in the winter time." But she commits suicide in the summer and under circumstances of horror which were fatal to the popular chances of the play. The scene was a bachelor flat at the very top of a high building close to the Albert Hall. The scene-painter and the lighting arrangements had managed to convey the impression of a cloudless golden day of summer. Through the windows of the sitting-room could be seen level with the flat the dome of the Albert Hall, and in the distance and far below the tops of the trees in Hyde Park. Outside the windows ran a balcony which served the two rooms. There was no way out of the flat at all except by the lift or the one staircase. Zoe was in this flat, when the sound of her husband's voice on the threshold sent her running into the bedroom. The husband and the commentator had called on the young man whom Zoe might or might not marry if she got a divorce or was divorced. Zoe's affairs were in an inextricable tangle. The husband and the commentator were to discuss the possibility of a reconciliation. The young man admitted that Zoe was in the flat, in the only other room in the flat. He opened the door and called to her. There was no answer. The husband imagined that she was up to some new trick. The young man standing in the doorway between the two rooms said in a voice of bewilderment, "I—I can't make it out. She's not there." C. M. Lowne, who was on the stage when the words were spoken on the first night, tells me that an audible shudder went through the house. For there was only one thing which could have happened. And there can be no death more shocking to the imagination than that of a woman who flings herself from the balcony as high as an eyrie to crash upon the stone pavement of a London square. If any words were needed to drive the horror home, there was the last line of the play to supply them, "She told me once it would be in the winter time".

The likelihood that *Mid-Channel* would appeal to a wide public was of course diminished by the absence of Alexander from the cast. He happened to have arranged a tour for this autumn, but when the director of a theatre is also its chief actor and produces a play in which he is not acting himself, a doubt is inevitably raised about the quality of the play itself. In this case there seems to have been some misunderstanding. For immediately before its production, Alexander is found writing to Pinero:

I have read the play again. I wish I had been able to read it months ago, for then I could have told you that I could play B. [Blundell] and serve you well. At our interview, you will remember, I asked you "What about the husband?" You said he did queer things. He is interesting, however, affords a great acting opportunity, and would have greatly added to my reputation as an actor. The play is a great tragedy, and will live when we are both cold. I am proud to think it is to be produced in my theatre. Bless you.

Yours ever,

ALEC

§

Apart from the production of *Mid-Channel*, the most noteworthy event in the record of the theatre during these years was the second revival of *The Importance of Being Earnest* on November 25th, 1909. The events which had so prejudiced the judgment of the public against the play were now far off. The publication of such a masterpiece as *The Ballad of Reading Gaol* had had an effect too upon men's minds. Indignation had softened into regret at the waste of a mind which had apparently not yet reached its highest power, contempt had shaded into pity. So, at last, the wittiest and the most joyous comedy of the generation came into its own. It was played for eleven consecutive months to crowded houses. Alexander, who had stood out of the cast of *Mid-Channel*, was once more John Worthing, the tearful mourner of his non-existent brother, and fortunately Allan Aynesworth was free to take up again the part of Algernon Moncrieffe and to resume over the muffins in the garden the debate on the morality of Bunburyism.

Allan Aynesworth played in nine plays at the St. James', and parts ranging from the artist in *The Prisoner of Zenda* to Gerald Harringay in *Liberty Hall*. But he was never better suited than in *The Importance of Being Earnest*. He had, natural to him, the finish of a light comedian of the first-class. He never took a sledge-hammer to drive in a bradawl; he knew just the strength of the tap which was necessary to send it home cleanly and neatly with one stroke. He had the quickness without hurry which those who had not watched the methods of John Hare, Charles Wyndham, Aynesworth, and Arthur Bourchier were accustomed to count the peculiar gift of the French comedians. He and Alexander together with Stella Patrick Campbell, Mrs Patrick Campbell's daughter, and Rosalie Toller in the place of Evelyn Millard and Irene Vanbrugh, E. Vivian Reynolds as Canon Chasuble, Helen Rous as Lady Bracknell, and Alice Beet as Miss Prism, gave a performance which did not fall behind the original presentation of the play.

The Importance of Being Earnest was still being performed when Alexander completed his twentieth year of management at the St. James' Theatre. On that anniversary he gave away to each member of the audience as a token of the occasion a specially bound copy of the printed play. He gave one to Allan Aynesworth with a letter written upon the flyleaf. From time to time one comes across foolish scraps of gossip which pretended that Alexander held himself aloof from his company and behaved

towards them with a haughty disdain. Any man who
has made any mark in the world must have sufficient
character to have made also a good number of
enemies and detractors, Alexander like the rest.
Nobody sets out to pull down someone who is on
the same level. He must be by a rung or two overhead before you can get a grasp of his coat-tails.
Alexander had many friends outside the circle of his
profession; he had a home life which occupied and
contented him; he was not a great frequenter of
clubs; he was naturally reticent and wore his heart
in its proper place instead of upon his sleeve. He was
not of the dear-old-boy school. He was certain,
therefore, to be charged with arrogance. But this
letter will give a truer and a more pleasant picture
of the relations which actually existed between
himself and those who worked with him:

My dear Aynesworth,

It is a pleasure to me to give you this little book in
remembrance of our friendship, and our happy and successful association as manager and actor. It will serve to remind
you, too, of your exquisite performance of "Algie", which
gave pleasure to the author, and the great British Public.

George Alexander
Feb. 1, 1910

Another instance may be recorded. In the autumn
of 1911 he produced a play called *The Ogre* by
Henry Arthur Jones. It was a satire upon the claims
of women. Playgoers may remember a scene in
which the man of the household, acted by Alexander,
nailed his riding-breeches, in place of a picture, above
his mantelpiece. It was that kind of satire. These

were the days of the militant suffragettes, of padlocks in Downing Street, and of the cat-and-mouse cure for hunger-strikes in gaol. Henry Arthur Jones was opposed to the movement. He was a genial, whole-hearted defender of lost causes. So he wrote this play *The Ogre*. It was meant to be a comedy, but it had to be played as a farce and even then it was not one of its author's many successes. I happened to drop into the theatre one evening whilst it was running and Alexander said to me: "I have got a young girl from the Gaiety in this play, who if she sticks to serious work is going to make a great name for herself. I'll take you round and introduce you."

He took me behind the scenes from his long dressing-room in the front of the theatre and pre-sented me to a lovely slip of a girl with a shining helmet of golden hair plaited and braided down over her ears—Gladys Cooper. She got her real opportunity a few months later in the last act of the play by Arnold Bennett and Edward Knoblock, *Milestones*, and with her native ability and beauty allied to hard work, shrewd common sense, and a strong character, she went forward from that moment until she reached her present commanding position upon the stage.

Alexander never grudged his praise when it was deserved. He was, I think, the least jealous man I ever knew. He never cut down another actor's opportunity lest he himself should be outshone. You were at liberty to act him off the stage if you could, and he would help you to do it, if so the play required; and as an actor he could afford it, for he was a very good actor with a very wide range from

farce to tragedy. Mannerisms? Well, yes! A twist of
the mouth, a bending of the knees—those were his
as other actors have others, and they would become
accentuated, if he was harassed, or his part was not
strenuous and left a corner of his mind free to worry
over some little problem which clamoured for a
solution. How good an actor he was was put to the
proof in 1911, the year of His Majesty's Coronation,
when on May 17th, at a gala performance of Bulwer
Lytton's *Money* given at Drury Lane, Alexander
acted the part of Alfred Evelyn. No bad actor could
make anything human of that preposterous and
theatrical prig, and few good ones. There was a
galaxy of stars gathered together in Drury Lane on
that night of May 17th, 1911. Sir John Hare resumed
an old part in Sir John Vesey, Graves was acted by
Sir Herbert Tree, Sir Frederick Blount by Cyril
Maude, Captain Dudley Smooth by Sir Charles
Wyndham, Clara Douglas by Irene Vanbrugh, Lady
Franklin by Winifred Emery, Georgina Vesey by
Alexandra Carlisle. Yet the performance which
secured the greatest praise from good judges was
the performance of Alfred Evelyn by George
Alexander.

The part of Alfred Evelyn is one of the longest
ever written, and for an actor accustomed to the
idiomatic dialogue of the authors of to-day the character, with its stilted phrases and exuberant speeches,
is as difficult to make tolerable as one can conceive.
Nothing but complete sincerity would do it. But
Alexander was an actor in whom complete sincerity
was an outstanding quality. He had the curious dual
gift of great executive art, the power to execute with

complete absorption, and the power to stand apart at the same time and criticise the execution. "To make Evelyn possible to-day", Henry Arthur Jones wrote to him on the morning after the performance, "is a great achievement". And Charles Wylie Mathews, Director of Prosecutions, himself the son of a great comedian and an inveterate playgoer, declared in a letter:

I hear nothing but the very highest praise of your performance of Evelyn. From everybody, and from none more than John Hare, has come the opinion that it was masterly, and, amongst the many good things, perhaps the best you have done. May I tender my sincere congratulations?

Yet another tribute came to hand from an acquaintance:

I hope you won't think me impertinent if I offer you my congratulations on your performance at Drury Lane.

One or two of your colleagues made no secret of the fact that they did not like their business, and I thought that one of them, at all events, played in that spirit: consequently you had more or less to carry the performance. It seemed to me that you did this with great gallantry.

These three letters were written by busy men, and busy men do not sit down to praise their fellow men, even though they be friends, without a strong conviction that the praise is deserved. A performance of the part of Alfred Evelyn—his intimate emotions displayed like lingerie in a shop window, his absurd test whether his friends liked him for himself or for his money bringing down the curtain of the third act upon a climax which is theatre and nothing but

theatre—would ruin the reputation of half the leading actors of to-day. For the man who could play
Aubrey Tanqueray, Hilary Jesson, and a score of
such characters, to attack without shrinking the
rodomontades of Alfred Evelyn, and to get away
with them was, as Henry Arthur Jones declares, an
achievement.

From the Ogre Alexander turned to an Ogress.
A novel by Robert S. Hichens, *Bella Donna*, had
achieved so much popularity that a villa was named
after it at Luxor. It was a story of an attempted
murder on the Nile amidst scenes of glowing colour
which R. S. Hichens had stippled point upon point
with all his meticulous care and luxuriance of phrase.
In transferring the novel to the stage a good deal of
the atmosphere was inevitably lost. The episode in
the desert on the edge of the Fayum, so important
in the book, disappeared. The characters became a
little thin. J. B. Fagan produced a workmanlike
rather than a colourful adaptation. But it *was* workmanlike; the dramatic moments of the story were
seized; Mrs Patrick Campbell played the part of
Bella Donna—reluctantly but well—she refused it
more than once and never liked it; Alexander himself
acted the Jewish doctor Meyer Isaacson, who frus-
trates the crime. There were some tense and effective
scenes and the play, though it could not be said to
add to Alexander's reputation, did nothing to detract
from it. *Bella Donna* ran for thirty-four weeks, from
December 9th, 1911, to August 1st, 1912; and, what
with the provincial tours and the crowded houses
at the St. James', became one of the greatest money-
making successes of the management.

§

Alexander, on the occasion when an album commemorative of his twenty-five years of management was presented to him on the stage of the St. James' Theatre on the afternoon of February 4th, 1915, dwelt with pride on the number of English authors whose work it had been his privilege to present. It was, indeed, a constant theme in the speeches he made and the interviews he gave. There were, however, two notable exceptions from his list of names: J. M. Barrie and George Bernard Shaw. Barrie's plays were presented as a rule by Charles Frohman, who was a theatre manager on both sides of the Atlantic. He was the lessee of the Duke of York's Theatre in London, and with what was practically a stock company, including Harry Irving, Gerald du Maurier, Irene Vanbrugh, and Dion Boucicault as producer. Alexander, however, had in his possession for a time one play by Barrie named *Two Kinds of Women*. There was a project to produce it at matinees with a star cast. But the project came to nothing and the play was subsequently placed in the evening bill at another theatre, under another title. I think it was under Arthur Bourchier's management at the Garrick Theatre that the play was seen, and that it was then called *The Wedding Guest*. But that is a conjecture.

With regard to George Bernard Shaw information is more positive. At some time during the run of *Bella Donna* Shaw and Alexander met between the acts. It must have been early during the run. Alexander asked for a play. Mrs Patrick Campbell wanted to play a cockney part. The suggestion must have happened to correspond with a theme which Shaw had already in his mind. For he began upon *Pygmalion* that very evening. By the month of June, the play was sufficiently complete for him to propose that he should read it to Alexander and Mrs Patrick Campbell. Apparently Alexander wished to hear it first of all by himself, and did so. He was delighted with the play, but was convinced that its success must depend upon the performance of the part of Eliza. He made a suggestion that that part could be played upon other lines than those upon which Shaw had worked. Shaw thought over the suggestion and disagreed with it. Anyone but Mrs Patrick Campbell would upset the balance of the whole play. If Eliza were watered down, Higgins would become a brute. The kind of bullying which was intended was that kind which is a way of making love. But the relations between Alexander and Mrs Patrick Campbell were now strained. They had been acting together throughout the run of *Bella Donna* and he definitely did not want to rehearse or act with her again. The plan, therefore, for the moment came to nothing. George Bernard Shaw expressed a hope that later on he might turn out something else for the St. James' Theatre, and Alexander replied with a grateful appreciation that the play had been read to him, and an admiration of the masterly way in which it had been read.

By this time the long run of *Bella Donna* had ended and the play now in the bill was a translation of *La Flambée*, a tense and stirring drama by Henry Kistemaeckers which had run for a year at the Porte

St. Martin Theatre in Paris. Ethel Irving, an actress
of appeal and force, had made a remarkable success
a year before in *The Witness for the Defence*. She had
left the company, before the run of the play was over,
to fulfil an engagement to tour in Australia. She had
now returned and in *The Turning Point*, as the
adaptation was called, she took the leading woman's
part. The character which Alexander played, that of
Colonel Felt, and hers, that of his wife, were both
of them strong and emotional. The couple had
drifted apart; he, an Officer of Engineers responsible
for some new fortifications on the frontier, had taken
to gambling, she to a lover. A tragic incident made it
essential that Colonel Felt should establish an alibi
and it was the wife only who could help him. Out
of this necessity came a renewal of passion and an
escape from the peril in which Colonel Felt was
placed. The two parts gave to their representatives
great acting opportunities and both actor and actress
made the most of them. Monsieur Kistemaeckers, who
was suffering acutely from rheumatism, was forbidden by his doctor to cross the Channel and attend
any of the early performances, but an account which
he received from an eye-witness filled him with joy
and he transcribed the account ecstatically:

During the intervals of the third performance at which
I was present, I caught the conversations of my neighbours.
The unanimous opinion was that Sir George Alexander
had revealed a power which made him actually England's
greatest actor and surprised even those who most appreciated
his fine talents. In the second act and in the third his art
reached a pitch which will draw all London. Since Irving's
day there has been nothing seen like it upon the boards.

The wariness of a biographer would naturally incline him if not to suspect altogether, at all events to repeat with hesitation, the transports of an author who receives an indubitable proof in the form of fees that his work has been acclaimed in a foreign land. But fortunately a hard-headed playgoer with a long and trained experience of men and letters has added his own unbiassed evidence. G. W. Smalley wrote to Alexander on the night when he saw the play:

My nerves are all unstrung after so many sensations and thrills and I nevertheless look back on my evening with pleasure; and on yours as a performance quite new to me and I thought to the house. The face was never more mobile; the expressions succeeded each other from one second to another, the differences clearly marked: the sum of the whole a complete record of emotions and mental processes.

You seem to have kept all the French text; which is perhaps too leisurely for the British mind and could be cut. But the stage handling of the whole left little room for criticism and the suspense lasted to the end. I should think you had a goldmine. Miss Ethel Irving had very fine moments and inspirations, and I thought I had never seen a piece more thoroughly rehearsed; the master hand in it all through.

The Turning Point ran through the autumn and into the new year of 1913. At the close of the run Alexander once again left his own theatre, this time to play at the Palace Theatre a one-act play written by Max Beerbohm, whose sharp and fastidious pen has been too seldom employed in the service of the stage. Alexander played in *A Social Success* for a month to the great pleasure of his audiences, and meanwhile produced at the St. James' Theatre a musical version

of the story of *Turandot*. Alexander drew a large fee
of £2400 for his month at the Palace Theatre. But
one must multiply that figure by two and a half
before one reaches the amount which *Turandot* en-
gulfed. It was a German medley by Karl Vollmoeller,
who with Reinhardt had enjoyed a success at the
Palace Theatre with a pantomime half melodrama,
half farce, and all fantastic, called *A Night in Venice*.
Turandot was gorgeously mounted, with Evelyn
D'Alroy in the title-rôle of the Princess, a long cast
and a much longer train of armoured warriors and
embroidered courtiers. It ran for twenty-seven performances to average takings of between £60 and
£70, and resulted in a loss of over £6000. No such
disaster had occurred before in the history of this
management, which was now nearing its twenty-fifth
year. Once only £3000 had been swallowed down
by the costly production of *Much Ado About
Nothing*. Twice £2500 had been lost. *In Days of Old*
and *The Eccentric Lord Combermere* were the unhappy occasions. But in the majority of the cases
where the balance was adverse, the loss was under
£1000. The Princess Turandot, however, was
notoriously a difficult person. Her three riddles had
cost the heads of a good many of the suitors for her
hand. It was in her tradition to penalise the manager
who provided her with a lodging. Karl Vollmoeller
was gracefully remorseful and thankful for the care
which had been lavished upon his work. Alexander
fell back upon a short revival of *Lady Windermere's
Fan*, and that play, with a comedy *Open Windows*,
by A. E. W. Mason, carried him comfortably to the
close of his season.

It was now the summer of 1913. During the past twelve months he had bought a meadow at Chorley Wood on the edge of the Common. There he had built himself a house and laid out a garden. It was furnished by this summer and for the rest of his life he and his wife made much use of it. It was a charming house, arranged with a separate suite of rooms for them on the first floor. It was within easy reach of the St. James' Theatre and gave them a greater privacy and fresher air than they could get in Pont Street, and the opportunity of welcoming their intimate friends to a place of quiet and rest.

He had been knighted in the summer of 1911, and on October 17th of 1912 he had conferred upon him the Honorary Degree of LL.D. at the University of Bristol. Lord Haldane of Cloan was the Chancellor, and amongst those presented to him with Alexander for the Degree were Sir Francis Younghusband, Sir William White, later the Director of Naval Construction, Sir Alfred Hopkinson, Vice-Chancellor of the University of Manchester, the Bishop of Bristol, and Earl Roberts of Kandahar.

Three years afterwards, when the war was at its height, *Pygmalion* cropped up again. The play had been done at His Majesty's Theatre with Sir Herbert Beerbohm Tree as Higgins and Mrs Patrick Campbell as Eliza. It had run for fifteen weeks with very great success, but it was more than possible that its appeal was not exhausted. A revival during the autumn of 1916 at the St. James' Theatre was considered. Bernard Shaw was cordial but in no hurry for a revival, and above all anxious that at this time of stress a play of his should not disappoint financially

LITTLE COURT, CHORLEY WOOD

a man with a theatre upon his hands. For whatever reason, Alexander let his theatre for the autumn and appeared only on January 25th, 1917, in *The Aristocrat*, a play by Louis N. Parker. He had the assistance of Genevieve Ward, Mary Glynne, Lennox Pawle, Charles Glenny, and young Dennis Neilson-Terry. This was the last play in which Alexander acted, and it is pleasant to record that it received the welcome and enjoyed the prosperity which attended upon the St. James' Theatre up to the outbreak of the war.

CHAPTER XII

The finance of the St. James' Theatre

Whilst Alexander was in his first year of management at the Avenue (now the Playhouse) Theatre, his manager bolted with the cash. He took what was in the till, £700, and retired to Mexico, where he remained for the rest of his life. To a young management, which if not still in long clothes was not yet upon its legs, the loss of so much money might well have been fatal. It was as bad as stealing a baby's arrowroot. It was natural therefore that, when Alexander moved on to the St. James' Theatre in the autumn of 1890, he should take steps to prevent a recurrence of such a disaster. The accounts were audited frequently, and a summary of each year's Profit and Loss was entered in a book from which the financial condition of the management could be read and estimated almost at a glance.

From this book quotations have already been made in reference to particular plays. But it may be of interest now to take a wider view and compare in slightly greater detail the continuous management possible for an actor in those days before the war with the in-and-out system which later conditions entail. For there are signs that the in-and-out system is coming in its turn to an end and that the actor-manager will be seen again sooner than seemed likely a year or so ago. The weekly expenses then were kept well within £900, and these expenses included not only the actor-manager's salary as an actor, but a sufficient proportion of the rent to enable the theatre to remain closed without loss during a reasonably long summer vacation and an annual reasonable outlay for repairs.

A vague phrase "overhead charges" is much in use in the theatres of to-day, and covers a whole crop of expenses which arise from multiple managements. Alexander held a direct lease from the owners. His business manager was directly employed by him and he was the only man responsibly employed upon the theatre's business. There was only one interest in the theatre, and there was therefore only one needed to safeguard it. The business manager had an adequate staff, but that staff was directly employed by Alexander. Salaries, of course, were lower; but it is a mistake to attribute the present rate of increase, as is so often done, to the insatiable demands of the actors. It is true that young people in every profession, actors like the rest, claim more opportunities of enjoyment and more of the modern facilities than their predecessors did. They want their small motor-cars and their golf-courses, and they are no longer content that acting should be their only form of exercise. A more spacious life is the proper aim of any man though he may be a little premature and impatient in demanding it. But there were other causes than a more modest scale of living which kept salaries at a lower level. Short runs make high salaries. A play before the war could be moderately successful. An actor could be acting for fifty nights where to-day he acts for five. There were, of course, complete fiascos in those days, but not so many. Then he could play cricket: now he must play tip and run. A continuous management meant very often continuity of employment; in play after play at the St. James' Theatre the same names recurred in the cast. Moreover the income-tax was lower. In the present practice, salaries are inevitably higher. In the actual production of a play in a theatre run by an actor-manager, the cost was less, for the scenery and furniture belonged to the theatre, accumulated as the number of the plays produced increased, and at a comparatively small expense could be altered and repainted to fit the proper setting of a new play. The result can be seen in such instances as the following. Alexander could produce an elaborate play like *The Turning Point* with a production cost of £1500, a lengthy cast which included, besides himself, Ethel Irving, J. D. Beveridge, Godfrey Tearle, Athol Stewart, and Lettice Fairfax, pay author's fees of £1300, and on a run of no more than a hundred and eleven performances, clear a net profit of £2561 and a florin. Of course he whipped his plays off before they began to lose the money which they had made. It is the great argument for a continuous management directed by an actor that he has plays which in an emergency can be revived, and it was better for author and actor-manager that a play should be capable of revival than that it should be killed outright by too prolonged an iteration. I am taking only the years between 1890 and the summer of 1914, the first twenty-four years of Alexander's management of the St. James' Theatre. For with the outbreak of war, circumstances so fantastic arose,

and so swiftly a new habit of mind became natural
to the people of England, that parallels between
those years of confusion and the equable smooth
years which preceded them are out of the question.
Comparisons of figures may be amusing but they
have no lesson.

Between then the first production at the St.
James', *The Idler* on February 26th of the year 1891
—*Sunlight and Shadow*, it should be mentioned, was
revived for three weeks from January 31st—and the
last before war broke out, a revival of *An Ideal
Husband* on May 18th, 1914, Alexander produced
twenty-seven plays which ended in loss. In three of
these, *Mollentrave on Women* by Alfred Sutro,
Mid-Channel by Arthur Pinero, and *Turandot* by
Karl Vollmoeller, he did not act himself. And without doubt, in a theatre conducted by an actor who
is to the knowledge of all playgoers his own leading
man, his absence from the cast is a serious handicap.
But there were twenty-seven plays which failed.
Yet in only one year of the twenty-four did he
manage and act for less than nothing. This was the
year lasting from the summer of 1894 to the summer
of 1895. His personal tour in the autumn of 1894 had
brought in a net profit of £2205 : 18 : 9, and his
touring companies a profit of £1298 : 17 : 5. In addition, he had let his theatre for a short time and received a rent of £448. But on January 5th, 1895, he
had produced *Guy Domville*, and on February 14th
The Importance of Being Earnest; on May 11th *The
Triumph of the Philistines*; on June 20th a revival of
The Second Mrs Tanqueray, and on July 4th a revival of *The Idler*. During that season he thus put on

three new plays and revived two old ones, with the result that, even counting in his salary and his private investments, there was a dead loss of £517 : 19 : 6. There were one or two other occasions when the profit on the year was entirely due to the Provincial Tour in the early autumn.

It is a common saying that the provinces, from the theatrical point of view, are dead; that the cinema has killed the touring companies; that only some huge revue with witty comedians, catchy tunes, and a kaleidoscope of flashing legs can hope to make both ends meet, and that only in a few towns. But is not that due to the extinction of the actor-manager, who, coming with the prestige of his theatre and his latest play, gradually built up for himself a following in the country, which looked upon his visit as one of the social events of the year?

Alexander's first tour, in 1891—a short one of five weeks—brought him a profit of £49; his second tour in 1892 of ten weeks, £467; his third tour of 1893, £2374. It is true that he had as his great attraction this year *The Second Mrs Tanqueray* in all its freshness. But the company was getting known for good plays, good acting, and good staging. It was acquiring a vested interest in the expectations of country playgoers. By the end of the century the autumn tours of twelve to fourteen weeks were bringing in, after all expenses had been paid, net profits of over £4000; and with the regularity of the returns from an investment in Government Stock. There are still some actors, like Matheson Lang and Martin Harvey, who, keeping their names known

by their periodic visits with excellent plays and
finished productions, reap their harvest in the provinces. But the background of the London theatre
and the London play is naturally of immense value;
and if the settled management returns in time to the
London stage, confidence in the provinces will be
restored and the popularity of the living play renewed.

The great profits, however, were made of course
in London. Up to the summer of 1914 Alexander
had put on at the St. James' Theatre twenty-six
successful plays and the returns from them were six
times as much again as his losses on the plays which
had failed. *His House in Order* stands at the head of
the list, and easily. It earned, clear of every expense,
£35,000. The much criticised *Bella Donna* came
next with £25,748. It is odd that *Bella Donna*, so
stripped of that gift for decoration which has made
its author famous, should come to so high a place
in the financial scale. *The Importance of Being Earnest*
came third. It brought £21,942 into the banking
account of the St. James' Theatre. It was followed
closely by *The Second Mrs Tanqueray*, which fell
short of that sum by £600. *The Thief* came fifth in the
list, Bernstein's play translated by Cosmo Gordon-
Lennox. Again it is strange that a play which has
made so small a stir in the dramatic history of those
twenty-four years should have earned more for the
theatre than either *The Prisoner of Zenda* or *Lady
Windermere's Fan*. But the cast was small, and since
the scenery required was not elaborate, it could be
sent on tour at a smaller cost. *The Thief* earned net
£19,460, *The Prisoner of Zenda* £18,132, and *Lady*

Windermere's Fan £15,631. All these sums, it should be understood, include the salary which Alexander paid himself as an actor both in London and the provinces. The net earning of those twenty-six plays amounted to a sum of £269,400 : 12 : 6.

LADY ALEXANDER IN THE GARDEN AT LITTLE COURT

CHAPTER XIII

Alexander's aims · The Memorial Theatre · The
censorship of plays · War work · His domestic
life · Its happiness

THERE are dreamers the very intensity of whose
dreams brings the imagined object nearer. George
Alexander was a man of immediate and definite aims
rather than of dreams. Far-off things, misty things,
things to be one day but not to-morrow, were for
other people. The idea of a great Shakespeare
Memorial Theatre in the heart of London which
should be the centre-piece of a free new drama was
making a good deal of noise in a small circle. But
the circle was widening. One large sum and some
smaller sums were collected; sites for the theatre
were debated; a treasurer was appointed; I have
heard one of the enthusiasts, Harley Granville-
Barker, suggest that the first Director should be
George Alexander, so sure did it seem to them that
the idea would soon become a fact. Alexander himself was lukewarm. He was not hostile, but the
idea was not near enough. On the other hand, when
the Shakespeare Tercentenary Commemoration Performance was proposed to take place in 1916, at
Drury Lane Theatre, no one strove more devotedly
to make it a success. For the presence of Their
Majesties the King and Queen, for an unequalled
entertainment, a souvenir programme illustrated by
famous artists, for all that could grace and make

memorable the occasion he gave untiring labour and thought. Here was something immediate and good, something notably worth while, to be done. He was as earnest as any enthusiast for the Memorial Theatre in a desire to make the drama a national possession of which a cultured people could be proud; and he did his best towards that end. But he did it in his own way, seeking a present and a visible advance. He used the St. James' Theatre. He threw open its doors to any kind of play. He never insisted that his part should be the best. He was willing to stand out of the cast altogether, and would have done so more often, had the authors of the plays been willing. He had confronted and overthrown a good deal of Puritanical hypocrisy when he staged *The Second Mrs Tanqueray*, and had by that act so raised the credit of the English stage abroad that the great actresses of France and Italy for the first time in many years turned their eyes towards England. For it should not be forgotten that in that year of 1893, when *The Second Mrs Tanqueray* was first produced, George Bernard Shaw was still with his name very much in the making.

Alexander was with his first London chief, Henry Irving, in upholding the dignity of the theatre, and brought to the work of upholding it the practical acumen which served him so well as a manager. The dignity of the theatre demanded that actors and actresses of experience and talent should not end in a poverty-stricken old age. He served for years on the Council of the Royal General Theatrical Fund, spoke or presided at its dinners, and became its President. He became President, too, of King

George's Pension Fund. When it seemed to him helpful, he became Vice-President of the Actors' Association. And when the West End Managers' Association seemed to be beating the air in 1914, he resigned from it.

In one respect he disagreed altogether with the forward school; and since he disagreed he fought. He was strongly for the retention of the censorship of plays. There had been cases in New York when the police had invaded a theatre and carted off the whole of the cast to the police station. He was afraid that if the censorship of plays were abolished, this might happen in some theatre, where a manager without a reputation and at his wits' end to keep going, had put on some noxious piece to obtain a success of scandal. There were more censorious people in those pre-war times. The good name of the stage would suffer, and it would not be saved because another author was treating somewhere else with an extreme bluntness of words and the most moral intention some difficult problem or malady of sex. The censorship was a protection, in Alexander's judgment, against both the scandal of an invading police and the scandal of a pornographic manager. The censorship of plays has ceased to be a subject of bitter controversy. It is used with a greater tact, a wider discretion. Plays once banned were seen not to be menaces to decency and sometimes were discovered to be of no great interest in themselves. The daring word became in time merely a vulgarity. It won't make a good play out of a bad play. If it's in keeping with the character represented, it is accepted. But as an audacity it cuts no ice. In those days bishops were mobilised to uphold the censorship; a Select Committee of the Houses of Parliament deliberated upon it; whether a spoken excess was more deleterious than a written one exercised this and that Association or Society. But out of the war there has come a greater liberality of thought due to a greater confidence that the inhabitants of the country may not know very much but are healthily sound in their judgments.

When the war came, therefore, it found in the chief actor of the St. James' Theatre a man trained by inclination and experience to do exceedingly well what was to his hand. He was fifty-six years of age with a wearing malady, a theatre upon his hands, and the theatrical industry looking to him for the mitigation of the difficulties which beset it. He did not spare himself. Through that first distracted year, he carried on the planned programme of his theatre at a heavy loss. Spy plays and revues ending with spectacular defeats of the Germans had it their own way. I remember seeing one in which the wife of the Governor of Gibraltar wandering casually in evening dress into a bar in Gibraltar at once unearthed a spy. Nothing was too ludicrous to be accepted, so long as it ended with the defeat of the Germans. Any other play must, in Pinero's phrase, be a play to scale mountains, if it was to succeed, and Alexander had no such play within his reach at the moment. He did what he could. He produced five plays between the autumn of 1914 and the summer of 1915, lost money on them all and acted in them all. Meanwhile, with the energetic assistance of Lady Alexander, he was continually organising matinées, arranging concerts, fixing up fêtes and garden parties, at the Temple, at the Albert Hall, anywhere, for the League of Mercy, for the provision of Homes for Officers' Widows, for the British Red Cross Society.

He had been President of the South Saint Pancras section of the League of Mercy, ever since his municipal connection with that constituency; his widow now holds that position, and between them they consistently supported it. But their chief endeavours were now given to furthering the work of the British Red Cross Society and of the Order of St. John of Jerusalem in England. He was elected, on the proposal of Her Royal Highness the Princess Christian seconded by the Hon. Charles Russell, a Member of the War Executive Committee, on May 19th, 1915, and immediately afterwards was appointed to the new Headquarters Collections Committee. He was one of the three members who attended the first meeting of that Committee which before the war was over had by the private efforts of its members collected £10,000,000 for the families of wounded and fallen soldiers. Whether sick or well, whether on holiday or at work, he devoted his time and his thoughts to it; and I have a note at my elbow from the chairman of the Committee informing him that as a result of an appeal which he had suggested to Executors of Estates, £10,000 had been given in one cheque.

By the autumn of 1915 the country had settled down methodically to see the war through. Pinero finished a comedy at which he had been working for the best part of two years, and Alexander was spared the constant rehearsal of new plays. *The Big Drum*, though not one of its author's sweeping successes, ran for sixteen weeks and was succeeded by a comedy called *The Basker* by Clifford Mills, which lasted for seventeen weeks and brought him to April of 1916. It was followed by *Pen*, a comedy by H. A. Vachell in which Alexander himself did not appear. A strong cast with Allan Aynesworth at the head of it interpreted the play, but it did not win the favour of the public, and once more no doubt the absence of the actor whose name was linked with the theatre in the minds of all playgoers prejudiced the chances of success. A revival of *Bella Donna*, however, in spite of a bitter attack upon the play in one newspaper, gave to his season a successful ending.

Alexander let the theatre for the autumn months, took a cure at Harrogate, and appeared at the Coliseum during the months of August and September. On January 25th, 1917, he produced his last play, *The Aristocrat*, by Louis N. Parker. It was a story of The Terror, that favourite subject of dramatists. Miss Genevieve Ward had in the course of it a startling moment, when, an old woman, she whimpered as she was led to the guillotine and then, recovering her pride, swept out to face the crowd. Alexander himself played brilliantly an exacting part, and the two young lovers of the play, the late Dennis Neilson-Terry and Mary Glynne, before the run was over made a reality of their impersonation.

The play caught on, and it was well that it did. For difficulties were now arising from Labour Restrictions and the needs of National Service all over the country, and Alexander's tact in mediation was being continually called upon and as continually lent.

GEORGE ALEXANDER IN *THE ARISTOCRAT*

The entertainment industry had somehow to be kept upon its legs. It was necessary to the spirit and the good cheer of the country for one thing, the chief thing. For another, the entertainment tax was a climbing asset in the resources of the Exchequer. But the loss of men in the great battles of Passchendaele and the Somme, and the vast increase in the output of munitions, made more and more demands upon the man-power of the country. Women and wounded men who had been discharged and men who were altogether unfit were in the main employed, but companies, like the Morecambe Town and Estates Company, Limited, which catered for the summer resorts needed a certain proportion of able-bodied men if they were to carry on at all. Compromises had to be reached. Men employed during the day on national work were allowed to work in theatres and pleasure-grounds after six. Men enrolled for national service were conceded the permission to engage without restriction in private work until the moment came when they were wanted. But these adjustments were not easy to make, so many needs must be co-ordinated, so many kinds of men brought to see the same thing with the same eyes. Meanwhile the Red Cross work went on. Meanwhile the theatre must be kept open.

After the summer of 1914 I saw very little of my friend. I was far away, and the mere fact that I could give myself leave hindered me from taking it. Once a year I came back for a few days to the Admiralty, and I was able to seek him out in the long room at the front of his theatre or pass the end of a week with him and his wife at his house of Little Court at

Chorley Wood. I saw him play the part of the Duke of Chastelfranc early in the run of *The Aristocrat*, and though he looked too finely drawn, he was buoyant and content, and happy in the work he did, whether in his theatre or on his many committees. He certainly needed a long holiday, but there were no signs of that fatigue or of that gradual narrowing of interests which are so often the prelude to the last illness. In the autumn, however, he was forced to resign his activities. Consumption saps the vitality secretly and at the end invades its weakened victim with an irresistible swiftness. The Bishop of London, an old friend, saw him in his bed at Chorley Wood on the afternoon of March 15th, 1918. Alexander recognised him and was even able to speak a few words of gratitude for his visit. But between midnight and 1 o'clock of the morning of the 16th he died peacefully at the age of fifty-nine.

He had lived a full, happy, enviable life. His wife was a constant helpmate and a good companion, watchful of his moods without appearing to be watchful, proud of him, clever in her management of his social affairs, and untiring. It was his habit to dine at half-past six in the evening before he went down to his theatre, and she always dined with him even though two hours later she had to dine again, or to have the appearance of dining again, in a house of their friends. If he was away from her on tour, he wrote to her each day, not a formal letter, but such letters as only people can write who are always in each other's thoughts. They were scribbled off anywhere on odd pieces of paper, in his dressing-room in the theatre, in the train. How he amused himself,

SIR GEORGE AND LADY ALEXANDER IN THE GARDEN
AT LITTLE COURT

what "the business" was like, who was playing against him in the particular town. If he had had a good dinner he told her so; when he won a round of golf—which was rarely—that went down too. A picture-postcard would be sent with the windows of his rooms marked with a cross. She would be told what the Mayor had said to him, and when he had a pint of champagne with his supper. She would be given commissions to carry out. The commissions might be simple, but it needed a lifelong devotion to decipher them. All trifles, no doubt, but trifles which mean a lovely and a pleasant companionship, inviolable by the years.

Alexander's pride and devotion were given to his theatre and its art and its growing importance in the eyes of thoughtful people. But he had a wealth of outside interests which kept his judgment sane, his sense of proportion as level as a compass-card. For instance, he was a Justice of the Peace of London; when he died he was Upper Warden of the Worshipful Company of Turners, and had he lived until May 9th he would have become its Master. As we have seen, politics municipal and imperial so engaged his mind that he took what part in them his strenuous busy life enabled him to do. But nothing, I think, did so much to make his life pleasant as his quick appreciation of the merits of others. He could squabble and quarrel and bluster on occasion like the rest of us, but of that brooding envy which cramps and disfigures so many natures there was never a sign. He was a warm and generous friend, doing his benefactions quietly, and writing them off as soon as they were done. The messages of condolence which were sent to his widow came from every quarter, from the Department of National Service to the Executive Council of the National Orchestral Association, from his old associates on the London County Council to the actors and actresses who served under him and with him. Of his private friends it is enough to say that all were made emptier of heart by his going and many of them emptier of hand. He carved out for himself a distinguished place in a crowded world and stood out as an example of the dignity of that calling which he was always swift to defend. On the completion of his twenty-fifth year of management, his comrades of the theatre presented to him a beautiful album in which had been mounted their tributes of admiration and love. Dame Madge Kendal made the presentation in a felicitous speech. It was the crowning moment of his career, and he treasured that book through the rest of his life as his widow treasures it now.

A NOTE BY LADY ALEXANDER

I feel a little shy at writing about myself, as it is difficult to divide our interests—we did everything together. It is especially difficult to follow the brilliant survey of my husband's work and character by Mr Mason. I find that there is very little for me to add to this wonderful book.

We had our ups and downs. All artistic natures are easily depressed, but we had a great many ups and very few downs. Mine is a sunny nature, and I always tried to keep Alec happy if possible. He always thought that I did not understand business and that I only thought of him and never of the future. He used to say, "Florence would be just as happy in a third-floor back with bread and cheese". Of course that was not true; I did care most awfully.

Our really great venture was going into management. We had not much money, so I made most of the dresses at home and I trimmed all the hats myself, and I really think they were quite nice.

First nights at the St. James' Theatre were great events. It was very nervy work for Alec with all the responsibilities he had in addition to acting his new part and remembering his words. I sat in my box sick with anxiety, and between the acts I used to put on an apron and go behind the scenes to place all the little things on the stage myself until the men got used to it. I arranged the flowers; in those days we had so much detail, and I loved to make things look real. I ordered the gowns to suit the decorations of the scene so that nothing clashed

227

or was ugly. Alec gave me the large sum of £5 a week for my work, and I think I was very cheap at the price.

Our first nights at the St. James' Theatre were like brilliant parties. Everybody knew everybody, everybody put on their best clothes, everybody wished us success. When I entered my box on a first night I always had a reception from the gallery. I do not know why, but I did. They were always so pleased and so kind to me.

When Alec first went to Irving as his leading man he was what they call a matinée idol, and Irving was too funny in trying to make him play costume parts. Alec was the smart young man about town. Irving once said to him, "Speak up, speak up to the little boy in the gallery who's paid his sixpence and probably got very wet waiting for his seat. Never mind the stalls, they can look after themselves, but never forget the little boy in the gallery." On another occasion Irving said, "Now, Alexander, not quite so much Piccadilly."

READ

One night in America Irving was playing Hamlet, and in the play scene the gauze caught fire on the stage and blazed up. The whole of the enormous audience rose and cried "Fire!" I was so frightened that I stood up and shrieked in a loud voice, "This always happens, it's part of the play". They did not know Hamlet *in those days so well as they know it now in America, and my cry saved the situation. Everybody sat down and said, "Part of the play". Irving went on acting the whole time and was very grateful to me for doing this. But when the curtain fell I had to creep out, as everybody was looking for me.*

Ellen Terry was a great help and a great friend to Alec. She taught him a great deal. He was quite a boy when he went to Irving, and Ellen Terry used to try and cure him of his nervousness. Her method was to drop things about the stage for him to pick up. He was terribly nervous and he used to get very upset, so he told Irving about it; but Ellen Terry would not listen, and I really think it was a great help to Alec later on.

Another good story of Ellen Terry is that she was to play in a Shakespearian play with him and she wanted £100 a week, not at all too much for her. She spoke rather shyly about this salary, and he turned round to her and said, "Oh, that's all right. You're a cheap dear."

His years with Henry Irving, who was a great and kind friend, were very successful.

Alec did not go out much to parties because of his work, but I did it all the time. I had no car in those days and the one bargain we had together was that no one was ever to see me home. I was very young at the time, and when I was dining out I had to dodge people in order to get away alone. Of course Alec had to keep late hours acting every night, and I made it a rule always to keep a servant up at night to have his supper ready and to put on his slippers. Alec had to dine at 6.30, so he was obliged to have supper after the theatre. I generally sat up for him, or if I was very tired I went to bed and then he had his supper in my room. He hated eating alone. Some people said I spoiled him, but I did not. He was much too good to spoil. I always tried to make his life perfect. Some actors' wives make the mistake of letting their husbands share the domestic worries. I kept every worry away from Alec that I possibly could. I used to run the theatre, my Pont Street house and my country house, and people used to say to Alec, "How does she do it?"

He would reply, "Oh, quite easily. I never hear any-thing about it." The actor-manager's life is a very difficult one. He hardly ever sees his friends, except at lunch time, for he is working when everybody else is dining.

In the early days we had a brougham, and I used to meet Alec after matinées. When I saw the charming girls crowding round the stage door to wish him good luck, I used to hide, for I had no wish to spoil sport.

At the theatre we had a wonderful staff. We had a housekeeper who was quite devoted to us. She was one of the old-fashioned servants who could make a brocade coat for The Prisoner of Zenda *or cook a lunch equally well, and her great pride was that she opened the door for Alec to go on the stage every day for twenty-five years.*

I would like to tell a story about a secretary we once had, for during the war we had a secretary. Alec sent all his people out to do war work, and ran the theatre with three or four people. He took the war very much to heart. This lady secretary was highly recommended to us. She used to come in to me each morning and say, "Sir George has given me a great deal of work to-day, and I shall have some difficulty in getting through it." I of course recognised that his work was the more important, so I gave her only one or two letters to write and said that would do for that day. The secretary then went to Sir George and repeated her story, this time saying that I had given her a great deal of work. This went on for two or three weeks, and at last Sir George came in to me and was very angry. "Look here," he said, "this must stop. This poor girl is being over-worked and I never can get anything done. You really must give her less to do." I was as much surprised as he was, and when I told him that I believed that he was overworking the girl we discovered that she had been going down to the theatre with only two or three letters to do and then going home, while we were both trying hard to keep pace with our correspondence.

I always attended the two last rehearsals before every play because my opinion was worth having just before the play was produced. My remarks were taken down in shorthand and I was always told I was wrong, but in the end my opinions were always taken and proved all right. When an actor has been rehearsing a play for weeks he becomes blind to its faults. I could say things to Alec about his work that nobody else could, and when I went in to the last rehearsals I was called the sledge-hammer.

I read a great many plays, and if one sent me to sleep and another woke me up I felt the latter was the play to produce. I had a great faculty for being able to tell Alec the plot of a play and to interest him enough to make him read it.

Alec always took off a play if the booking was not good ahead. But he could always run a play for a month because he had a large clientele who never missed a play that he did, and that kept him going until his new play was ready. His admirers never let him do a play without seeing it.

We had wonderful friends like Sir Alfred and Lady Fripp. The Duke and Duchess of Fife, Princess Arthur and Princess Maude were frequent visitors to our house at Chorley Wood, and they were most kind friends. They were very encouraging to Alec and came to our first nights at the St. James' Theatre, proving *most splendid judges of plays. Mr Percy Macquoid did a great deal of work for us, more particularly in Paolo and Francesca, which he made a most beautiful production.*

Our only real quarrels were when Alec would over-work. I did my best to make him rest when he was playing long parts. Many times when we have been in hotels I have sat outside the door to prevent people from making a noise when he was resting, though he did not know it. But wives are the last people husbands will listen to about resting. I always remember that Lord Dawson of Penn saw him when he was not well and ordered him three months' rest, which of course he would not take. During the war the Red Cross were very anxious to send Alec to settle some disputes in Salonika. I begged him to go, and I firmly believe that if he had gone and done one thing—for he hated acting during the war—instead of overworking as he did, he would have lived. But he was over-persuaded not to go. My own war work was selling programmes for every matinée and every charity for the war, and I got many thousands of pounds. Sometimes people would give me £20 for a programme. The public were most generous, and it was as easy to collect money then as it is difficult now. I used to send in large sums all the time, and I have obtained as much as £700 for programmes in one evening.

When we were in Berlin, two years before war broke out, we were being entertained by all the German theatres. We arrived very late one night in Berlin and the next morning the Kaiser sent a letter by hand asking Alec to go and act before him a fortnight later and bring his own company. Without any hesitation Alec refused as he had a play coming on and he could not spare the time. I was afraid all day long that we should be arrested. Of course we ought to have gone to the British Ambassador and consulted him; but all was well, and Alec was always delighted in after years that he had not complied with the Kaiser's request.

Alec used to marvel that I could go and sit through a play night after night and still enjoy it. He said I was such an admirer of his. I always preferred seeing him act to anybody else. He was a very modest man, and always thought that everyone was more clever than he was. I had to buck him up. I once heard a very funny story. I liked to sit in the stalls and hear the remarks. A certain Duchess in London was so pleased with his acting that she took off her tiara and threw it in admiration at his feet! Of course I demanded the tiara when I saw him. But some of the stories one hears are very remarkable.

When we first married I used to make my own gowns, much to Alec's surprise as they were mostly pinned together, but the effect was quite good. I was rather "extreme" with clothes on the stage, for in those days people went to see the St. James' plays before ordering a new gown.

Alec was always so very unselfish, and he really hastened his end by overwork. When he felt ill he never would give himself a chance, and he would not listen to me. He took very few holidays, as he kept the theatre open for eleven months of the year. He always said he could not afford to take longer holidays, and he kept his staff on while the theatre was closed. He loved Little Court. We built it for rest, but I am afraid he took very little rest there, for he used to bring his

County Council work and his plays to study on Sunday, which I resented very much.

When an author read a play to him I was always present, and the author used to try to flatter me by saying, "If Lady Alexander would play this part——"
Alec used to get up and say, "When she goes on the stage I go off." I thought it much better for him to remain on the stage, so I did not accept these offers from authors.

Alec's motto was

> "Do thy duty, that is best,
> Leave unto thy God the rest."

It was written in all his little day-books.

FLORENCE ALEXANDER

June 27, 1935

APPENDIX A

LIST OF PLAYS PRODUCED BY SIR GEORGE ALEXANDER AT THE ST. JAMES' THEATRE, AND DATES OF PRODUCTION

SUNLIGHT AND SHADOW, a play in 3 acts, by R. C. Carton (transferred from the Avenue Theatre)	31st Jan. 1891
THE GAY LOTHARIO, a play in 1 act, by Alfred C. Calmour	31st Jan. 1891
THE IDLER, a play in 4 acts, by C. Haddon Chambers	26th Feb. 1891
MOLIÈRE, a play in 1 act, by Walter Frith	17th July 1891
LORD ANERLEY, a play in 4 acts, by Mark Quinton and Henry Hamilton	7th Nov. 1891
FORGIVENESS, a play in 4 acts, by J. Comyns Carr	30th Dec. 1891
LADY WINDERMERE'S FAN, a play in 4 acts, by Oscar Wilde	20th Feb. 1892
MIDSUMMER DAY, a play in 1 act, by Walter Frith	30th March 1892
KIT MARLOWE, a play in 1 act, by W. L. Courtney	31st Oct. 1892
LIBERTY HALL, a comedy in 4 acts, by R. C. Carton	3rd Dec. 1892
THE SECOND MRS TANQUERAY, by Arthur W. Pinero	27th May 1893
THE MASQUERADERS, a play in 4 acts, by Henry Arthur Jones	28th April 1894
GUY DOMVILLE, a play in 3 acts, by Henry James	5th Jan. 1895
TOO HAPPY BY HALF, a comedy in 1 act, by Julian Field	5th Jan. 1895

235

The Importance of Being Earnest, by Oscar Wilde   14th Feb. 1895

In the Season, a play in 1 act, by Langdon E. Mitchell   14th Feb. 1895

The Triumph of the Philistines, by Henry Arthur Jones   11th May 1895

The Misogynist, a play in 1 act, by G. W. Godfrey   23rd Nov. 1895

The Divided Way, a play in 3 acts, by H. V. Esmond   23rd Nov. 1895

The Prisoner of Zenda, by Anthony Hope and Edward Rose   7th Jan. 1896

As You Like It, by William Shakespeare   2nd Dec. 1896

The Princess and the Butterfly, or The Fantastics, a comedy in 5 acts, by Arthur W. Pinero   29th March 1897

The Tree of Knowledge, a play in 5 acts, by R. C. Carton   25th Oct. 1897

Much Ado About Nothing, by William Shakespeare   16th Feb. 1898

The Conquerors, a drama in 4 acts, by Paul M. Potter   14th April 1898

The Ambassador, a comedy in 4 acts, by John Oliver Hobbes   2nd June 1898

A Repentance, a drama in 1 act, by John Oliver Hobbes   28th Feb. 1899

In Days of Old, a romantic drama in 4 acts, by Edward Rose   26th April 1899

Rupert of Hentzau, by Anthony Hope   1st Feb. 1900

The Man of Forty, a play in 4 acts, by Walter Frith   28th March 1900

A Debt of Honour, a play in 5 acts, by Sydney Grundy   1st Sept. 1900

The Wisdom of the Wise, a play in 3 acts, by John Oliver Hobbes   22nd Nov. 1900

The Plot of his Story, a play in 1 act, by Mrs Oscar Beringer   22nd Nov. 1900

The Awakening, a play in 4 acts, by C. Haddon Chambers   6th Feb. 1901

The Wilderness, a play in 3 acts, by H. V. Esmond	11th April 1901
Old Crimea, a play in 1 act, by Cosmo Hamilton	11th July 1901
A Patched-up Affair, a play in 1 act, by Florence Warden	7th Jan. 1902
Paolo and Francesca, a tragedy in 4 acts, by Stephen Phillips	6th March 1902
If I were King, a play in 4 acts, by Justin Huntly M'Carthy	30th Aug. 1902
Old Heidelberg, a play in 5 acts, by Wilhelm Meyer-Forster and Rudolf Bleichmann	19th March 1903
Love's Carnival, a play in 5 acts, by Erich Hartleben and Rudolf Bleichmann	17th March 1904
Saturday to Monday, a comedy in 3 acts, by Frederick Fenn and Richard Pryce	14th April 1904
'Op o' Me Thumb, a play in 1 act, by Frederick Fenn and Richard Pryce	25th April 1904
The Garden of Lies, a romance in 4 acts, by Justus Miles Forman and Sydney Grundy	3rd Sept. 1904
The Decree Nisi, a play in 1 act, by Joshua Bates	18th Oct. 1904
A Maker of Men, a play in 1 act, by Alfred Sutro	27th Jan. 1905
Mollentrave on Women, a comedy in 3 acts, by Alfred Sutro	13th Feb. 1905
How he Lied to her Husband, a play in 1 act, by Bernard Shaw	21st March 1905
John Chilcote, M.P., a play in 4 acts, by E. Temple Thurston and Katherine Cecil Thurston	1st May 1905
The Man of the Moment, a play in 4 acts, by Henry Melvill, Alfred Capus, and Emanuel Arène	13th June 1905
His House in Order, a comedy in 4 acts, by Arthur W. Pinero	1st Feb. 1906
John Glayde's Honour, a play in 4 acts, by Alfred Sutro	8th March 1907

THE THIEF, a play in 3 acts, by Henry Bernstein and Cosmo Gordon-Lennox	12th Nov. 1907
THE THUNDERBOLT, a play in 4 acts, by Arthur W. Pinero	9th May 1908
THE BUILDER OF BRIDGES, a play in 4 acts, by Alfred Sutro	11th Nov. 1908
COLONEL SMITH, a comedy in 4 acts, by A. E. W. Mason	23rd April 1909
THE NURSERY GOVERNESS, a play in 1 act, by M. Provins and P. G. Duchesne	3rd May 1909
MID-CHANNEL, a play in 4 acts, by Arthur Pinero	2nd Sept. 1909
LORRIMER SABISTON, DRAMATIST, a play in 3 acts, by R. C. Carton	9th Nov. 1909
D'ARCY OF THE GUARDS, a play in 4 acts, by Louis Evan Shipman	27th Sept. 1910
ECCENTRIC LORD COMBERDENE, by R. C. Carton	19th Nov. 1910
THE WITNESS FOR THE DEFENCE, a play in 4 acts, by A. E. W. Mason	1st Feb. 1911
THE OGRE, a play in 3 acts, by Henry Arthur Jones	11th Sept. 1911
THE MINIATURE, a play in 1 act, by Walter Frith	Oct. 1911
BELLA DONNA, a play in 5 acts, by Robert Hichens and James Bernard Fagan	9th Dec. 1911
THE TURNING POINT, a play in 3 acts, by Henry Kistemaeckers and Peter Le Marchant	1st Oct. 1912
TURANDOT, PRINCESS OF CHINA, by Karl Vollmoeller and Jethro Bithell	18th Jan. 1913
OPEN WINDOWS, a play in 3 acts, by A. E. W. Mason	11th March 1913
PLAYGOERS, a play in 1 act, by Arthur Pinero	31st March 1913
THE ATTACK, a play in 3 acts, by Henry Bernstein and George Egerton	1st Jan. 1914
THE TWO VIRTUES, a play in 4 acts, by Alfred Sutro	5th March 1914

AN IDEAL HUSBAND, a play in 4 acts, by Oscar Wilde — 14th May 1914

THOSE WHO SIT IN JUDGMENT, a play in 4 acts, by Michael Orme — 19th Sept. 1914

KINGS AND QUEENS, a play in 3 acts, by Rudolf Besier — 16th Jan. 1915

THE PANORAMA OF YOUTH, a play in 4 acts, by J. Hartley Manners — 14th April 1915

THE DAY BEFORE THE DAY, a drama in 4 acts, by Chester Bailey Fernald — 19th May 1915

THE BIG DRUM, a play in 4 acts, by Arthur Pinero — 1st Sept. 1915

THE BASKER, a comedy in 4 acts, by Clifford Mills — 6th Jan. 1916

PEN, a comedy in 3 acts, by Horace Annesley Vachell — 3rd May 1916

THE ARISTOCRAT, a play in 3 acts, by Louis N. Parker — 25th Jan. 1917

SHEILA, a comedy in 3 acts, by Githa Sowerby — 7th June 1917

A SOCIAL SUCCESS, a play in 1 act, by Max Beerbohm — 27th Jan. 1913 Palace Theatre

APPENDIX B

LIST OF PLAYS PRODUCED AT THE ST. JAMES' THEATRE BY SUB-LESSEES DURING SIR GEORGE ALEXANDER'S TENANCY

Mr William Elliot's Season—

BOGEY, a play in 3 acts, by H. V. Esmond   10th Sept. 1895

Mr and Mrs Kendal's Seasons—

THE ELDER MISS BLOSSOM, a comedy in 3 acts, by Ernest Hendrie and Metcalfe Wood   22nd Sept. 1898

THE LIKENESS OF THE NIGHT, a play in 4 acts, by Mrs W. K. Clifford   28th Oct. 1901

DICK HOPE, a play in 3 acts, by Ernest Hendrie   16th Sept. 1905

THE HOUSEKEEPER, a farce in 3 acts, by Metcalfe Wood and Beatrice Heron-Maxwell   12th Oct. 1905

Mr E. S. Willard's Season—

THE CARDINAL, a play in 4 acts, by Louis N. Parker   31st Aug. 1903

TOM PINCH, by J. J. Dilley and Lewis Clifton   5th Sept. 1903

THE PROFESSOR'S LOVE STORY, a play in 3 acts, by J. M. Barrie   7th Dec. 1903

Mr William Mollison and Miss Lilian Braithwaite's Season—

BESIDE THE BONNIE BRIAR BUSH, by Ian Maclaren, Augustus Thomas and James Macarthur   23rd Dec. 1905

AS YOU LIKE IT, by William Shakespeare   9th Jan. 1906

Mr Edward Compton's Season—

> THE 18TH CENTURY, a play in 3 acts   29th July 1907
> THE SCHOOL FOR SCANDAL, by Richard   14th Sept. 1907
> Brinsley Sheridan

Mr Forbes-Robertson's Season—

> THE PASSING OF THE THIRD FLOOR BACK,   1st Sept. 1908
> by Jerome K. Jerome

Mr F. R. Benson's Season of Christmas Matinees—

> THE PIPER, by Josephine Preston Pea-   21st Dec. 1910
> body

Lillah McCarthy and Granville Barker's Season—

> THE HARLEQUINADE, by Dion Clayton   1st Sept. 1913
> Calthrop and Granville Barker
> ANDROCLES AND THE LION, by Bernard   1st Sept. 1913
> Shaw
> THE WITCH, a play in 4 acts, by H. Wiers-   29th Oct. 1913
> Jensen and John Masefield
> THE WILD DUCK, by Henrik Ibsen   1st Dec. 1913
> LE MARIAGE FORCÉ, by Molière   2nd Dec. 1913
> NAN, by John Masefield   2nd Dec. 1913
> THE DOCTOR'S DILEMMA, by Bernard   6th Dec. 1913
> Shaw
> THE DEATH OF TINTAGILES, a play in 5   17th Dec. 1913
> scenes, by Maurice Maeterlinck and
> Alfred Sutro
> THE SILVER BOX, by John Galsworthy   18th Dec. 1913

Mr Matheson Lang's Season—

> THE MERCHANT OF VENICE, by William   1915
> Shakespeare

Alfred Butt's Season—

> PEG O' MY HEART, by J. Hartley   May 1916
> Manners

Edwin T. Heys' Season—

LUCKY JIM, a play in 3 acts, by Henry   19th Oct. 1916
   Seton

CHARLEY'S AUNT, by Brandon Thomas   14th Dec. 1916

INDEX OF NAMES

THE END

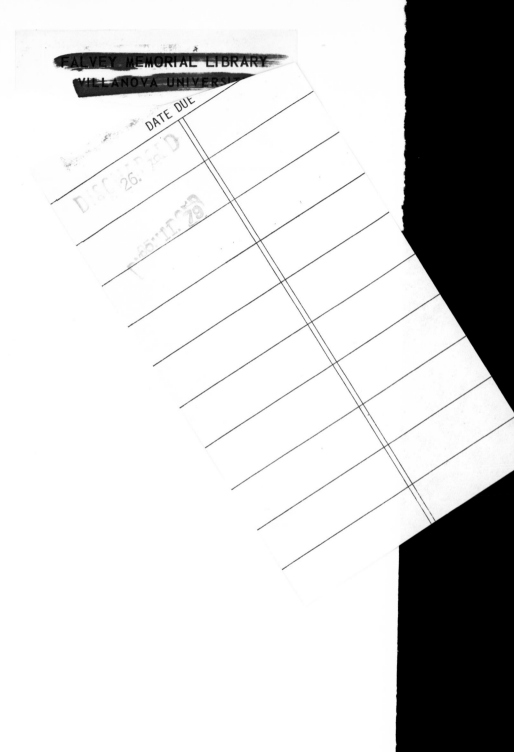